STUDIES IN HISTORY, ECONOMICS AND PUBLIC LAW

Edited by the

FACULTY OF POLITICAL SCIENCE OF COLUMBIA UNIVERSITY

NUMBER 475

ADVERSITY'S NOBLEMEN

BY

CHARLES TRINKAUS

ADVERSITY'S NOBLEMEN

The Italian Humanists on Happiness

BY

CHARLES TRINKAUS

1965

OCTAGON BOOKS, INC.

New York

Reprinted 1965
by special arrangement with Charles Trinkaus

OCTAGON BOOKS, INC.
175 FIFTH AVENUE
NEW YORK, N. Y. 10010

LIBRARY OF CONGRESS CATALOG CARD NUMBER: 65-25895

Printed in U.S.A. by
NOBLE OFFSET PRINTERS, INC.
NEW YORK 3, N. Y.

PREFACE TO RE-ISSUE OF 1965

Adversity's Noblemen was written in the late 'thirties and originally published in 1940 by Columbia University Press. It is now being re-issued by Octagon Books by means of the photo-offset process, so that only a few important corrections and an errata-list are permissible. Therefore some sort of "Retractationes" or Retrospect after twenty-five years seems essential.

An historian who did not regard the re-issue of his first publication after twenty-five years with some degree of mixed feelings and misgivings would be foolhardy, indeed. Such feelings are especially appropriate in this present instance. Renaissance studies in America were at a low point in 1940, but now they are flourishing with a much more expert and sophisticated scholarly community engaged in their pursuit. They have experienced their own "Renaissance".[1]

Moreover, this book was written at a time when the "revolt"[2] of American medievalists against Jacob Burckhardt's image of the Renaissance was at the peak of its influence. Perhaps Charles Homer Haskins' *The Renaissance of the Twelfth Century*[3] and my own teacher, Lynn Thorndike's *Science and Thought in the Fifteenth Century*[4] contributed most to forming a counter-image of a flourishing medieval learning and a declining, amateurish intellectual effort in what came to be called "the so-called Renaissance". Further influences that were disparaging to a positive view of the Renaissance were the publications of Étienne Gilson, including the English version of his *The Spirit of Medieval Philosophy*[5] in 1936, and the publication of Jacques Maritain's *True Humanism*[6] in 1938—books which reinforced a spreading current of neo-Scholasticism in American academic circles. In 1939 Douglas Bush stressed the "fundamentally medieval" character of Renaissance humanism in his *The Renaissance and English Humanism.*[7]

One effect of the scholarly hostility to the once solidly established view of the Italian Renaissance was the spread of an interpretation of Burckhardt's position which was at least exaggerated and at worst distorted. My own researches into late medieval "pessimism", begun in Professor Thorndike's seminar, had turned up a lengthy collection of gloomy pronouncements about the times, about man, about life. When I decided to limit my explorations of "pessimism" to Italian humanism in writing this book, I took it for granted that I would find in Burckhardt's *Civilization of the Renaissance* a perfect target of untenable assertions. In fact, as my first chapter shows, I was unable to find this generally attributed point of view in Burckhardt, and I began to think of the concept of an Italian Renaissance, and of humanism, as not so historically indefensible as the anti-Burckhardtian historiography had suggested. I am happy to have had the opportunity subsequently[8] to state more adequately my appreciation of this great nineteenth century historian and thinker than I had in my treatment of him in this book where I initially sought to emphasize differences.

I found, moreover, that I was dependent upon Burckhardt and in agreement with him with respect to his firm insistence on individualism in the Renaissance generally and in the humanists in particular. Where I differed, and would still to some extent do so, was in viewing this individualism as necessarily optimistic. I did not accept his estimate of the boldness and self-confidence of the men of that age. Here it would be a matter primarily of degree of emphasis, for I soon discovered that a positive, hopeful outlook was most definitely present in the Renaissance and among some of the humanists. I recognized the truth of this in this book, although, admittedly, more begrudgingly than I would today. And Burckhardt, for his part, perhaps saw the dark side of the Renaissance more emphatically and was much more seriously and critically concerned about it for what it spoke concerning the contradictions of the modern life-situation than a less profound reading of history than his own might recognize. Moreover, I changed the subject of my own investigation from "pessimism" to the humanists' views of happiness, which was a much more inclusive and less one-sided approach. But I still stressed the negative aspects of the humanists' positions, as is reflected in the title: ADVERSITY'S NOBLEMEN.

Burckhardt's interpretation of the Renaissance was far more psychological, social and moral than it was political, economic or intellectual. My own interest in the Italian humanists in this book necessarily also (because of the theme of happiness) became concerned with their psychological response to their social experience as stated and evidenced in their moral-philosophical treatises. Subsequent to 1940 one of the dominant modes of interpreting Renaissance humanism, in what some of its proponents regard as a vindication of Burckhardt's essential view,[9] is an emphasis on "civic humanism". The leading exponent of "civic humanism" in America has been Hans Baron who began developing this point of view in Germany in the late 'twenties and brought it to completion with the publication of his two volumes, *The Crisis of the Early Italian Renaissance*[10] in 1955. I had found his work, and particularly his article on "Franciscan Poverty and Civic Wealth",[11] of the utmost value to me in writing this book, as its pages reveal. I have the deepest respect for his integrity and imaginative scholarship. But I found it necessary to differ with him in this book on one essential point, and I would continue to do so today.[12]

My position, briefly, is as follows: "Civic humanism", without any question, was a very important aspect of Italian humanism and of the Renaissance, but it was neither an exclusive kind of "humanism" nor the essence of humanism or the Renaissance. I am far more inclined today than I was in 1940 to emphasize the importance of the conception of learning, culture and education as responsive and responsible to the civic community as an inherent feature of the rhetorical tradition in western civilization from the Greek Sophists to the Renaissance humanists. It is undeniable that a stress on the civic role of culture was a recurrent and central facet of Italian humanism.[13] Baron, and some of his followers, however, while rightly grasping the importance of this aspect of humanism, to my mind fail to give adequate recognition to another, more introspective, contemplative and self-concerned side of humanism. It is true that this side of humanism is accepted by Baron as characteristic of the "medieval" fourteenth century humanists who lived before the great Florentine triumph of 1402. He also thinks of the contemplative, self-concerned aspect of humanism as reappearing in the late Quattrocento after the downfall of Florentine republicanism, among "courtiers and humanistic litterati" of the Medicean circle.[14] What I would insist on, however, is that humanism in its broad scope (not just "civic" humanism) really does find its beginning in the mid-fourteenth century with Petrarch and his associates (and perhaps even earlier in Padua, Arezzo and Florence), that both an emphasis on civic responsibility and an emphasis on contemplative inwardness or social withdrawal seem to have been present to some degree at all periods of its history, and sometimes in the same individual. Petrarch is regarded by Baron as non-civic-minded,[15] but Petrarch also had his moments of civic-concern and certainly regarded his humanistic activities as directed toward moral improvement.[16] On the other hand, Poggio Bracciolini, who served as Florentine chancellor and was a close associate of Bruni and other indisputably "civic" humanists, did not always share their confidence in the value of civic activity; in fact, in many of his writings he was a profoundly pessimistic and inward man.[17] Moreover, a sense of civic responsibility does persist in many humanists associated with the later Ficinian Neoplatonic circles.[18]

I have no serious quarrel on this aspect of the question with Eugenio Garin, perhaps the leading contemporary Italian Renaissance historian, who sees a blend of spirituality and moral activism widely spread through the Renaissance, and does not try to encapsulate "civic humanism" quite so severely within narrow chronological limits. But Garin also is sometimes inclined to speak slightingly of humanists who were pure scholars or philosophers who seemed comparatively indifferent to the civic responsibilities of men of learning.[19] For my part, while I recognized in this book the unadulterated "civic humanism" of Leonardo Bruni and to a slightly lesser extent that of Giannozzo Manetti (and the very positive and self-reliant individualism of Lorenzo Valla) and tried according to my lights to give a balanced point of view, I would today include other figures. In general I now recognize that there was a more widespread this-worldly optimism, particularly among the Florentine citizen-humanists of the first two thirds of the Quattrocento. But I would not abandon my thesis that the self-image of a substantial number of Italian humanists could be characterized as ADVERSITY'S NOBLEMEN.

A more compelling question has been raised by Lauro Martines in his recently published book, *The Social World of the Florentine Humanists*.[20] Martines has given, in several respects, a more moderate and historically sound version of Baron's thesis concerning "civic humanism", and has supplied detailed evidence from the Florentine archives proving the unsuspected wealth of a large number of Florentine humanists and their close personal connections with the city's powerful political figures during the first half of the Quattrocento.[21] My implicit assumption of personal material want or even poverty on the part of some of these humanists must certainly be modified in the light of Martines' researches, although this would not change what I believe to be a fact, namely that there was a deep sense of insecurity in the writings of several of them and that not all of them, by any means, regarded their own situation complacently. What puzzled Martines was that although I acknowledged and was aware that some of the figures I treat in this book were men of substantial background or wealth, I still could argue that they were insecure.[22] I would repeat this argument because my interpretation was and would still be essentially moral and psychological, rather than economic or political. But I would certainly agree that this welcome accession of information concerning the material and political standing of the Florentine humanists should be taken into account, as prior to Martines' book it could not. I would wonder, however, whether it is legitimate to assert, as Martines does,[23] that "In part, in large part, the force of humanism in the Florentine community was the disguised force of the ruling class itself." Some of these humanists, unquestionably one like Leonardo Bruni, may have reflected or even voiced the proud sentiments of self-conscious confidence in the political and cultural achievements of the leading citizens on behalf of the Florentine commune. But to be of a leading family, to hold office, to conduct a business and participate in public affairs was to belong to a social, political and economic status which in early Quattrocento Florence meant to belong to the "ruling class". To be a humanist did not mean to belong to the "ruling class", even though, on Martines' showing, a remarkable number of such leading citizens who clearly constituted the "ruling class" also engaged in humanistic activities in varying degrees and even admitted many leading humanists of humbler origin to the privileges, rewards and responsibilities of the "ruling class". Humanism was a learned profession and a cultural movement which, however favored by those of high social status, should not be confused with high social status.[24] The thinking and the subjective attitudes of humanists were necessarily shaped by other forces, deriving from their intellectual tradition and their growing knowledge of a wide range of ancient moral, social, philosophical and religious ideas, besides the inducements of high material status earned by their activities or conferred on them by admiring associates of the "ruling class" and by the communal political organs which they controlled.

If these leading citizens-become-humanists and their honored professional humanist friends shared moments of proud optimism stemming from their affluence and civic achievements, apparently both groups were also subject to equally-shared moments of doubt. At least this is what Gene A. Brucker, a distinguished historian of Florence and a close scholarly associate of Lauro Martines has recently suggested. In an article on "The Structure of Patrician Society in Renaissance Florence"[25]

Brucker asserts that Florence in the Renaissance was governed by a tension between two social forces: a new, capitalistic, wealth-accumulating individualism and the old medieval corporate structure which survived in a newly transformed version. The latter institutions were seriously weakened, however, by the dynamic pattern of new individuals rising and falling in the social, economic and political hierarchies. The old corporate sources of security and status were no longer effective either for maintaining one's relative social position or for blocking the rise of new rivals. As a consequence the individual found himself in a newly exposed and insecure situation and turned for protection and assistance to the "neo-feudal bonds" of dependence on the most powerful of the patrician families. "In this society," writes Brucker, "in which corporate groups had lost much of their power and cohesiveness, the individual was extremely vulnerable. He was no longer protected, to the same degree as before, by family or guild connections."[26]

Thus the conclusions I suggested were implied by the treatises that are the subject of this book find an interesting confirmation in these views of Brucker. His conclusions are based, not on an examination of the tone, passimistic or otherwise, of the humanist treatises on happiness and human destiny, but on his close study of the archival material from which he derived his extensive knowledge of Florentine society and politics in the fourteenth and early fifteenth centuries.[27] And these feelings of insecurity are seen by Brucker, not as confined to one group such as the humanists, but as extending throughout the community and including even the patricians.

Brucker is critical of Burckhardt's view of Renaissance individualism as optimistic. "In his description of social change in the Renaissance, Jacob Burckhardt argued that the individual had become emancipated from the corporate bonds of the medieval world, that he had become a free man in a free social order. . . . But contradicting the vision of Renaissance man joyfully breaking his traditional bonds and exulting in his liberty is the picture of the Florentine who desperately sought new

sources of security and identity to replace those which had disappeared."[28] Brucker's interpretation may be compared to the
earlier one of mine, especially pages 39 to 41 and 144 to 147
of this book. If in Florence, as Martines has shown, the humanists were less separated from and hostile to leading citizen circles than I had supposed, it now seems likely, in accordance
with Brucker's views, that they also shared much of the uncertainty and foreboding of these same circles, in addition to their
moments of confidence. Certainly there seems to have been a
sufficiently frequent sense of gloom and insecurity to justify
their designation as ADVERSITY'S NOBLEMEN.

An interesting case in point is the relationship between a
young and not very affluent humanist, Bartolommeo della
Fonte, and his mentor and patron, Donato Acciaiuoli. Donato,
as is well known,[29] came from an old and distinguished Florentine family, served prominently in government offices and
embassies, and was Gonfaloniere della Giustizia in 1474. Moreover, Donato was one of the more influential citizen-humanists
in Florence in the 'sixties and until his death in 1478 with a
high reputation for his Aristotelian studies begun under Johannes Argyropoulos. Della Fonte (or Fontius, as he was generally known), born in 1446, seventeen years younger than
Donato, has left a remarkable account of his own "adversities"
and of how the humanist studies were urged upon him by Donato as a spiritual remedy for his material uncertainties and
difficulties. It is in a letter written the 26th of August, 1472,[30]
apparently his twenty-sixth birthday, in which he reviews and
evaluates his previous life and determines upon his future
course. It is addressed to his most intimate friend, the Florentine humanist and copyist, Pietro Cennini.[31] Turned away from
humanistic studies at the age of fifteen in order to support
younger siblings, resuming his humanist studies and activities
at twenty-two, experiencing one set-back and difficulty after
another, he was eventually taken along by Donato Acciaiuali
on a diplomatic mission. There complaining to him, "that these
times are so adverse to learned men that I would gladly ex-

change the study of humanity and eloquence for more profitable although lesser trades . . .",[32] he provoked Donato to make the following pronouncement:

"It is my duty, because of my great love for you, to counsel and warn you not to give up in the middle, in order that, if I can be of any help, I do not appear to have been remiss in urging it upon you, and if I should now be of less benefit, at least after this you will know that my intentions were high. Very frequently thinking over what put you in this state of mind, I see but two causes, the pursuit of wealth or of vulgar honors. But is it right, for the sake of some inane little glory and for sordid gain, to lose those immense riches which, while you are alive, are never snatched away from you, nor their praise even when you are dead? Do you not know that all things seated in the power of fortune are fleeting and un-stable, and that these things, both while men are seeking them and after they have acquired them, are subject to a thousand unpredictable chances? What, I ask, is more distinguished than to adhere, not to heaping up riches, not to acquiring false honors, but to the understanding and knowledge of many and great things? Everything else is vain and mutable and more onerous than honorable to its holders. Virtue alone is eternal and delightful and useful to its possessor. And only the studies of wisdom, instructing us in righteousness and virtue, consoling in adversity, adorning in prosperity, warn-ing faithfully what is to be sought and what avoided, lead us to true praise and glory. Indeed, on the contrary, popular favor and the desire for wealth both in the seeking weary our souls by the hope of gaining them and, once acquired, so disturb us by the fear of losing them that we find no peace in these things. Since, moreover, of the things that exist some are in our power and others are located beyond our power, it is the mark of an insane man to presume that things that are not his in his own right are in his power, or to think that those which are his own are alien. Moreover, to desire, assent, choose, decline, prepare, discern are in our own control; but glory, strength, beauty, wealth and other things of that sort which we are more able to wish for than to get for ourselves are alien to us. Of the things whose choice is in your power you ought to choose whatever is most useful, and the most useful to you, indeed, is to live rightly, far from the maddened crowd. But you cannot do that unless you cultivate the mind properly. Hence you must give yourself totally to those arts by which you are able most rightly to educate it. And since for living well precepts and instructions that lead to happiness are necessary, which are everywhere gathered from our studies, it is worthwhile to devote yourself to these studies; in pursuing them you may even expose the soul to gain and honor. Do you not know that Leonardo and Poggio acquired perpetual fame and virtuous riches by this one faculty of speaking and writing? Did our Scala ascend by any other route than this to wealth, honors and dignities? Therefore let us bestir ourselves, and if somewhat less than we are able, still more than we are doing, let us take up and come to the assistance of the now almost reviving eloquence according to our strength."[33]

These may not have been the exact words of Acciaiuoli, but they are presumably a close paraphrase, and in a letter as personal as this one to a most intimate friend, the sentiment may be taken as genuine. Here the leading "civic-humanist" of his generation, and certainly both a statesman and scholar who was looked to for scholarly and moral guidance by many of the younger generation of humanists,[34] departs from the usual image of him as the Aristotelian moralist counseling an active life to deliver a neo-stoic sermon on the value of the humanities as a consolation for the defeats and adversities of a worldly life. To the threats and uncertainties of "fortune" are opposed the "virtues" acquired through the *studia humanitatis*. His pronouncement supplements and confirms the interpretation offered in this book.

But, as the closing sentences of his statement indicate, there is no apparent conflict between shunning the pursuit of external goods and gaining the honest honors typified by the three humanist chancellors of Florence that he mentions: Leonardo Bruni, Poggio Bracciolini and Bartolommeo Scala.[35]

Fontius, himself, who never did gain the wealth, honors and public dignities of these others, although he had the deep respect of his contemporaries for his scholarship, concluded his own account of his new resolution to pursue the *studia humanitatis*, cost what they may, as follows:

"Miserably disturbed by these exhortations, and after I returned to the city repeating them to myself very often, I went back wholeheartedly to our common studies. Let some, in order to gain riches, navigate even as far as Britain. Let others, to acquire some dignity, wait before the doors of the powerful. For my part, content with poverty, having removed ambition and avarice, whatever time is left from the care of necessary affairs I would bestow on our studies."[36]

In this mood Fontius, too, conceived of humanism as a means to become one of ADVERSITY'S NOBLEMEN.

A venture into the question of the relationship of a movement of thought to contemporary living conditions and social structures is always hazardous and problematical. But some assumptions and regularities with regard to this relationship at any given time seem essential to the tasks historians propose for themselves. Whatever contribution this book has made (or failed to make) toward a greater awareness of these assumptions, it has at least discussed a central tenet of the Burckhardtian image of the Renaissance and provoked a more searching examination of the life situation of the Florentine humanists. And it does seem clear that the pursuit of humanistic studies was, in the minds of the humanists themselves and of their contemporaries, intimately connected with the problems of earthly, urban existence. Only some of the time, and with some humanists, these studies were considered an important means to advance public civic values; at other times, and with other humanists, they were regarded as an anodyne and alternative to the harshness and insecurity of participation in economic and political life.

To my mind the value of this study may well lie in its consideration of the different genres of moral philosophy within
which the humanists discussed the questions of the goals and
conditions of human life, in the analysis of the range and character of the underlying positions they took on these questions
within these genres, and in the identification of the classical,
patristic and medieval traditions on which they drew. A recon-
sideration of the entire question of "happiness", which other
commitments now make impossible, would attempt to relate the
humanists' positions much more specifically and concretely to
these classical sources and to the patristic and medieval Christian discussions of the question. One such study of a single
humanist—Klaus Heitmann's *FORTUNA und VIRTUS,
Eine Studie zu Petrarcas Lebensweisheit*[37]—is a model in many
respects (although he does not always base his arguments on
the most compelling evidence in Petrarch and does not discuss
Petrarch's moral philosophy as in any way connected with his
life-experience). Particularly valuable is Heitmann's demonstration that both adverse fortune and prosperity were regarded
as menacing to the individual's moral integrity and were to be
combatted by the opposing but complementary themes of "the
dignity and excellence of man" and "the misery of the human
condition", respectively. Moreover, his analysis of the complexity of Petrarch's oscillations between a Stoic-ascetic attitude and a Christian-Neoplatonist (and sometimes even a Peri-
patetic) frame of reference is salutary in establishing Petrarch's
relationship to classical, patristic and medieval traditions. My
own recent study of "Humanist Treatises on the Status of the
Religious: Petrarch, Salutati, Valla",[38] on their attitudes
toward the medieval, monastic alternative to worldliness, also
stressed their tendency to arrive at a new position which was a
blend (but in each case a unique blend) of the classical and
Christian traditions.

Despite the evidences of similarity to medieval attitudes that
this book, perhaps superficially, suggests, my present views of

Renaissance humanism would strongly emphasize its distinctive and progressive character.[39] In drawing on Christian, as well as classical, traditions the humanists decisively favored the patristic over the medieval phases of Christianity. As I indicated in chapter 2, the approach of St. Augustine was much more compatible with that of the humanists than the approach of St. Thomas Aquinas. In rejecting the scholastic and other medieval positions (though surreptitiously borrowing from them), the humanists did not in the least believe that they had broken with the Christian tradition. But in favoring the patristic model of how to blend Christianity and classical thought,[40] they inevitably evolved unique positions of their own in keeping with their own age and its problems.

Moreover, the humanists manifested, as Burckhardt insisted, individualism, but an individualism that was attuned to the outlook and situation of their own time rather than the far more secularized political and economic individualism[41] of the last two centuries. It was an individualism that could be introspective and pessimistic as well as active and affirmative. This humanistic individualism found expression in many studies and activities that, although they were far more secular than those of medieval scholars and writers, still remained within the context of a Christian vision of life. Humanistic individualism manifested itself in many bold acts, statements and ideas, as Burckhardt claimed, but it also retreated into the traditional and conservative paths that were available from the older institutions and patterns of ideas which were still part of the historical environment. The humanists discovered many new ways of being bold and original in statement, literary form or idea in the classical literary and philosophical works that they unearthed, translated and came to know in decisively new accuracy of detail and comprehensiveness. But they also found in these same classical sources many of the same ideas and passages that had illuminated or given structure to medieval thought.[42] As Wallace Ferguson has argued, it was an age of "transition",[43] with elements of novelty and uniqueness and elements of tradition and convention. The two together, and the underlying existential situation that provoked and incited them, mixed with and reacted upon each other to produce the historical distinctiveness of Renaissance culture. This is what I hoped to show through this book twenty-five years ago in 1940. With the modifications suggested above, and not without the greater misgivings of greater awareness of complexity, this is what I still want it to show today.

FOOTNOTES for PREFACE TO RE-ISSUE OF
ADVERSITY'S NOBLEMEN

1. It would be inappropriate to offer a complete bibliography of Renaissance studies written by Americans over the last twenty years, as well as impractical because of its length. The few titles listed here are merely a fragmentary indication of some of the more influential or representative publications. They are in chronological order, rather than by authors: Wallace K. Ferguson, *The Renaissance in Historical Thought,* Cambridge, Mass., 1948; E. Cassirer, P. O. Kristeller, J. H. Randall, Jr. eds., *The Renaissance Philosophy of Man,* Chicago, 1948; Myron P. Gilmore, *The World of Humanism,* New York, 1952; Hans Baron, *The Crisis of the Early Renaissance,* Princeton, 1955; P. O. Kristeller, *The Classics and Renaissance Thought,* Cambridge, Mass., 1955; Garrett Mattingly, *Renaissance Diplomacy,* Boston, 1955; B. L. Ullman, *Studies in the Italian Renaissance,* Rome, 1955; Ernest Hatch Wilkins, *Studies in the Life and Works of Petrarch,* Cambridge, Mass., 1955 (and his other Petrarch studies); P. O. Kristeller, *Studies in Renaissance Thought and Letters,* Rome, 1956; Eugene F. Rice, Jr., *The Renaissance Idea of Wisdom,* Cambridge, Mass., 1958; Theodor E. Mommsen, *Medieval and Renaissance Studies,* Ithaca, 1959; Marvin B. Becker, "The Republican City State in Florence: An Inquiry into its Origin and Survival (1280-1434)," *Speculum,* 1960 (and his other studies); J. H. Randall, Jr., *The School of Padua and the Emergence of Modern Science,* Padua, 1961; Bernard Weinberg, *A History of Literary Criticism in the Italian Renaissance,* Chicago, 1961; Gene A. Brucker, *Florentine Politics and Society, 1343-1378,* Princeton, 1962; Lauro Martines, *The Social World of the Florentine Humanists, 1390-1460,* Princeton, 1963; B. L. Ullman, *The Humanism of Coluccio Salutati,* Padua, 1963; Felix Gilbert, *Machiavelli and Guicciardini,* Princeton, 1964. This list, it should be noted, includes no publications in the history of the art, which have been massive, nor in the history of science, nor musicology, both significant.

2. It is significant that Ferguson, *op. cit.,* ends his history of Renaissance historiography prior to 1948, the date of its publication, with a chapter entitled, "The Revolt of the Medievalists. The Renaissance Interpreted as Continuation of the Middle Ages." (Chapter XI, pp. 329-385). The previous chapter (X, pp. 290-328) was called "Reaction Against the Burckhardtian Tradition: The Origins of the Renaissance Thrust Back into the Middle Ages."

3. Cambridge, Mass., 1927.
4. New York, 1929.
5. New York, 1936.
6. New York, 1938.
7. Toronto, 1939.
8. In an "Introduction" to the Harper Torchbook edition of Burckhardt

of 1958, written with Benjamin Nelson.

9. Cf. Hans Baron, "Burckhardt's *Civilization of the Renaissance* a Century after its Publication," *Renaissance News,* Vol. XII, No. 3 (Autumn, 1960), pp. 207-222: p. 222, "It is in association with the increased attention now paid to sociological factors that the core of the Burckhardtian conception of the Renaissance can carry full conviction for a reader of today. In this metamorphosis, Burckhardt's view proves equal and may still, eventually, prove superior to the competing views about the nature of the transition to the modern age." However, it needs to be said that Baron's chief criticism of Burckhardt, offered earlier in this paper, relates to Burckhardt's admiration of individualism as the chief source of Renaissance culture and to his emphasis on an antagonism between the individual and the civic community. (Cf. pp. 217-220) "Civic humanism" must in certain respects, therefore, also be regarded as a thesis contrary to Burckhardt's. My own approach has, of course, been more sympathetic to this aspect of Burckhardt's interpretation of the humanists.

10. *Op. cit.*

11. "Franciscon Poverty and Civic Wealth as Factors in the Rise of Humanistic Thought," *Speculum,* XIII (1938), pp. 1-37. Cf. this book, pp. 16-17, 57, 78, 85, 87, 112, 118-119.

12. This book, p. 78 and n. 134. Cf. my review of his *The Crisis of the Early Italian Renaissance,* in *Journal of the History of Ideas,* Vol. XVII, No. 3 (1956) pp. 426-432, espec. pp. 430-431 for my views and criticisms.

13. Cf. a recent attempt to summarize this question in my article, "Humanism", *Encyclopedia of World Art,* New York, 1963, cols. 702-743, section headed: "Moral and religious concerns of the humanists," cols. 717-720.

14. Baron, "Franciscan Poverty and Civic Wealth," *op. cit.,* p. 26.

15. *Ibid.,* p. 12.

16. Cf. Francesco Petrarca, *De Viris Illustribus,* edizione critica per cura di Guido Martellotti, Volume Primo, Firenze, 1964, *Prohemium,* p. 4, "Apud me nisi ea requiruntur, que ad virtutes vel virtutum contraria trahi possunt; hic enim, nisi fallor, fructuosus historicorum finis est, illa prosequi que vel sectanda legentibus vel fugienda sunt . . ." This passage stating the purpose of his most important historical writing was cited by the late Theodor E. Mommsen. Mommsen has made Petrarch's moral committments and his more than anticipations of the position of later humanism very clear in three papers republished in his *Medieval and Renaissance Studies, op. cit.:* pp. 106-119, "Petrarch's Conception of the Dark Ages;" pp. 130-174, "Petrarch and the Decoration of the Sala Virorum Illustrium in Padua"; and pp. 175-196, "Petrarch and the Story of the Choice of Hercules." The passage cited on p. 174 differs slightly from the text above because Mommsen was using the old edition of De Nolhac.

17. Cf. this book pp. 53-56, 87-90, 124, n. 9 and passim.

18. My study, "A Humanist's Image of Humanism: The Inaugural Orations of Bartolommeo della Fonte," *Studies in the Renaissance,* VII (1960), pp. 90-125 showed the extent to which he regarded the *studia humanitatis* as

contributing to the community. "Fontius" who is quoted below lived between 1446 and 1513. P.O. Kristeller has recently emphasized Bartolommeo Scala's concern for ways humanists might contribute to public office. Cf. his "An Unknown Correspondence of Allessandro Braccesi," *Classical, Medieval and Renaissance Studies in Honor of Berthold Louis Ullman*, Rome, 1964, pp. 311-342, espec. pp. 334-341. On Scala as author of a *Historia Florentinorum* and a dialogue *De Legibus et Iudiciis* cf. Felix Gilbert, *Machiavelli and Guicciardini, op. cit.* pp. 209, 215, 219, 222, 318-19; Nicolai Rubinstein, "Bartolomeo Scala's Historia Florentinorum," *Studi in Onore di Tamaro de Marinis*, Verona, 1964 Vol. IV, pp. 49-59. Eugenio Garin regards the humanists in the Florentine chancellery at the time of Lorenzo the Magnificent as no longer significant as political thinkers but as mere courtiers. Cf. his "I cancellieri umanisti della Repubblica Fiorentina da Coluccio Salutati a Bartolomeo Scala," *La Cultura filosofica del Rinascimento Italiano*, Florence, 1961, pp. 3-27, espec. pp. 26-27. Gilbert, however, stresses the importance of the continuity of relationship between humanists and office-holding as one of the conditions for the emergence of the political maturity of Machiavelli and the historical maturity of Guicciardini, this despite their break with certain humanistic rhetorical conventions.

19. Cf. his *L'Umanesimo italiano: filosofia e vita civile nel rinascimento*, Bari, 1952. And Garin particularly distrusts humanists of the Laurentian era.

20. *Op. cit.*

21. Cf. chapters 3, 4 and 5, and especially Appendix I, "Forty-five Profiles of Men Connected with Florentine Humanism."

22. *Ibid.*, pp. 92-93. I was certainly in error when I suggested on page 50 that Buonaccorso da Montemagno lacked wealth or social standing, but I was quite aware of the professional success of Salutati and Poggio, of the high social position of Manetti and Pico. On pages 78 and 79 I discussed the discontent of wealthy humanists as psychological and moral rather than due to "their economic dependence and insecure social place" as charged by Martines. But see my further comments in this introduction.

23. *Ibid.*, p. 270 and the entire section 3, "The Social Basis of Humanism" of chapter 7 which provides the context of this statement.

24. If at times in this book I seem to be guilty of the same fallacy of confusing a social and economic status with a cultural and intellectual movement, the reader should be clear that today I would resolve the question in favor of separation. This does not mean that the problem of the *inter-relationship* between cultural movements and environmental social structures is not one of major importance.

25. In *Colloquium, A Journal of Historical and Social Thought*, Ed. Norman F. Cantor, No. 1, April, 1964, pp. 2-11.

26. *Ibid.*, p. 9.

27. *Op. cit.* in note 1.

28. *Colloquium* article, *op. cit.*, p. 11.

29. Martines, *op. cit.*, pp. 348-349.

30. Bartholomaeus Fontius, *Epistolarum Libri III*, Ed. Ladislaus Juhász,

Budapest, 1931, Lib. I, Ep. 18, pp. 15-18. The letter is dated VII Cal. Septembris MCCCCLXXII. On p. 16 Fontius says, "Caeterum cum ad hunc meum natalem diem, quo sextum et vigesimum annum ingredior, totius ante actae vitae rationem reddiderim, cur modo ad intermissa studia toto animo me converterim, quam brevissime potero, enarrabo." The difficulty is that, if Fontius was born in 1446 (cf. my study of Fontius, *op. cit.,* p. 91, n. 4), this would be his twenty-seventh year that he was entering, although his twenty-sixth birthday, the probable basis of his confusion. Incidentally, it has not been noticed that the date of this letter seems to give the date of his birth.

31. On Cennini cf. B.L. Ullman, *The Origin and Development of Humanistic Script,* Rome, 1960, pp. 123-126. On Fontius' intimate relationship with him, cf. C. Marchesi, *Bartolomeo della Fonte,* Catania, 1900, pp. 20-24.

32. Fontius, *op. cit.,* pp. 16-17, "haec tempora doctis esse hominibus tam adversa commutaturumque me libenter, si versura fieri posset, humanitatis et eloquentiae studia cum quaestuosis quanvis minoribus artibus affirmavi...."

33. *Ibid.,* pp. 17-18, "Officium meum est pro meo summo in te amore tibi consulere et monere, ne medio in spatio cursum sistas, ut, si quid prodesse queam, non videar mea cohortatione defuisse, ac, si minus nunc profuero, saltem posthac intelligas mihi voluntatem egregiam affuisse. Ego vero mecum persaepe reputans, quid in istam te mentem impulerit, nullas, nisi duas causas esse video aut divitiarum aut vulgarium honorum assequendorum. Sed an decet pro inani quadam gloriola et pro sordido quaestu eas immensas opes amittere, quae vivo tibi nunquam adimentur, neque earum laus mortuo quidem? An ignoras, quae in fortunae arbitrio sita sunt, fluxa et instabilia cuncta esse, quae, et dum homines quaerunt, et postquam adepti fuerint, mille incertis casibus submittuntur? Quid porro praeclarius est, quam non struendis opibus, non falsis honoribus exquirendis, sed multarum magnarumque rerum cognitioni et scientiae inhaerere? Caetera omnia vana et fluxa sunt habentibusque magis oneri quam honori. Virtus sola aeterna est et iocunda et utilis possidenti. Sola etenim sapientiae studia nos ad honestatem et virtutem instituentia in adversis rebus consolando, in prosperis adornando, quid sequendum, quid vitandum sit, fideliter emonendo ad veram laudem et gloriam nos perducunt. Contra vero aura popularis ac divitiarum cupiditas et quaerendo habendi spe fatigant animos nostros et quaesita amittendi metu ita solicitant, ut in eis nullam quietam reperiamus. Quando autem eorum, quae sunt, alia in nostra, alia extra nostram potestatem locata sunt, insani est hominis, quae sui iuris non sunt, in potestate sua esse praesumere, aut, quae propria sunt, aliena existimare. Nostrum est autem appetere, assentiri, eligere, declinare, praeparare, decernere; alienum gloria, robur, pulchritudo, divitiae caeteraque id genus, quae magis optare, quam vendicare nobis valemus. Sed earum rerum, quarum te optio penes est, cum eligere utilissimam quanque debeas, utillimum vero procul insania vulgi recte vivere tibi sit, id autem facere nequeas, nisi animum bene colas, iis artibus totum dedere te debes, quibus illum quam rectissime possis excolere. Sed cum ad bene vivendum sit opus praeceptis et institutis ad felicitatem ducentibus, quae undique ex nostris studiis colliguntur, operae est pretium, his incumbas, in quibus etiam prose-

quendis si [sic] lucro animum et honori subiicias. An Leonardum Poggiumque ignoras hac una dicendi scribendique facultate sibi perpetuum nomen et honestas divitias comparasse? An alia, quam hac duce Schala noster ascendit ad opes, ad honores, ad dignitates? Quare age, expergiscamur aliquando minusque nobis, quam possumus, plus tamen, quam facimus, assumamus ac iam prope reviviscenti eloquentiae pro virili nostra subveniamus."

34. This same Fontius wrote a treatise in dialogue form, called, *Donatus, sive de poenitentia* in which the principal spokesman was Donato Acciaiuoli in the role of the pious counselor of the young Fontius seeking his views on penance. (Cf. Wolfenbüttel, Cod. 43 Aug. Fol., ff 118v-140v and other MSS and editions cited in my Fontius Study, *op. cit.,* pp. 128-129.) Giovanni Nesi, the young Neoplatonic humanist, prophet and follower of Savonarola, uses Acciaiuoli as the spokesman for his exposition of secular ethics in his *De Moribus* (Florence, Bibl. Laurenziana, Pl. LXXVII, cod. 24, ff. 9r et sequ.).

35. There apparently was no discrimination either as to distinction or merit between the first two and Scala in the eyes of Fontius, or of Acciaiuoli, although Eugenio Garin feels that with Scala "Il cancelliere è un funzionario, non è più né un grande esponente politico né un gran letterato." "I cancellieri umanisti della Repubblica fiorentina," *op. cit.,* p. 27. But see Kristeller, "An Unknown Correspondence of Allessandro Braccesi", *op. cit.* p. 337, n. 3 for Cardinal Ammannati's view of Scala as inferior to none of his predecessors in the chancellery.

36. Fontius, *op. cit.,* p. 18, "His ego adhortationibus et tunc miserabiliter sum commotus et iisdem, postquam in urbem redii, mecum saepius repetitis totum ad communia studia me converti. Alii, ut divitias cumulent, Britannos usque adnavigent. Alii ante potentiorum fores excubent, ut assequantur aliquam dignitatem. Equidem paupertate contentus ambitione avaritiaque semota omne tempus, quod a rerum necessariarum cura supererit studiis nostris impertiar."

37. Studi Italiani namens des Istituto Italiano di Cultura in Köln herausgegeben von F. Schalk und M. Marianelli, Band 1., Köln und Graz (Böhlau Verlag), 1958. My own study: "Petrarch's Views on the Individual and His Society," *Osiris,* vol. XI (1954), pp. 168-198, based solely on the *Secretum* and the *De vita solitaria,* sought to examine his psychological and moral views in relation to his experience. The relationship of humanist moral thought to earlier traditions has been the particular concern of P. O. Kristeller. Cf. his "Humanism and Scholasticism in the Italian Renaissance," *Studies in Renaissance Thought and Letters, op. cit.* pp 553-583; *The Classics and Renaissance Thought, op. cit.*; and more recently, "The Moral Thought of Renaissance Humanism," pp. 20-68 of his *Renaissance Thought II,* New York, 1965.

38. *Studies in the Renaissance.* Vol. XI (1964), pp. 7-45

39. I use the word "progressive" in the same sense that art historians call painters "progressive" who arrive at imaginative new solutions of problems confronting their predecessors, without any political implication or content.

40. Cf. P. O. Kristeller, "Augustine and the Early Renaissance," *Studies*

in Renaissance Thought and Letters, op. cit., pp. 355-372. My own current researches in Italian humanist religious thought lead me to even stronger insistence on the pervasive influence of Augustine on the humanists. In some respects it might even be claimed that the humanists understood his thought for the first time, since they like him were confronting the issue of the relationship of Christianity to pagan, classical and secular culture with peculiar intensity. One of Eugenio Garin's most important papers has been on patristic influence on humanism: "La 'Dignitas Hominis' e la letteratura Patristica," *La Rinascita,* I, 4 (1938), pp. 102-146.

41. It would be the purport of Martines' book that the humanists, since they fused so nearly totally with the political and economic elite of Florence, did practice economic and political individualism. I would rather emphasize that their economic activities were limited and their political initiative, even as Chancellors, unproven, but that their moral, political, literary and historical ideas and expression manifested great initiative and originality even where they made heavy use of classical sources.

42. The humanists were not at all cut off from medieval traditions, really, but they viewed these in very new ways, as they also viewed in new and historically more authentic ways the same classical sources that were utilized in the Middle Ages.

43. Cf. his *Europe in Transition,* Boston, 1963.

ERRATA

ON:	FOR:	READ:
p. 44, l. 4	Antonio Panormità.	Antonio Beccadelli, il Panormita.
p. 45, l. 1	(Bartolommeo de Sacchi)	(Bartolommeo Sacchi)
p. 49, n. 34, l. 5	eruditia	eruditio
p. 67, n. 87, l. 4	sequestrio	sequestratio
p. 67, n. 88, l. 3	terrestia	terrestria
p. 74, n. 118	dotore	dolore
p. 75, n. 120, l. 10	objectis velaminibus.	abiectis velaminibus [cooperiret].
p. 77, n. 132, l. 7	Viti	Vite
p. 82, l. 30	Panormità	Beccadelli, il Panormita
p. 90, n. 25, l. 3	referendum	resecendam
p. 90, n. 25, l. 4	vite	vitae
p. 91, n. 32, l. 2	pecunia	pecuniae
p. 91, n. 32, l. 3	monstra	monstro
p. 94, n. 42, l. 2	molestis	molestiis
p. 96, n. 51, l. 6	institutit	instituit
p. 97, n. 56, l. 1	voluptas	voluptates
p. 98, n. 59, l. 3	tardisculus	tardiusculus
p. 103, n. 83	*Prohemium,* II,	*Prohemium,* I,
p. 103, n. 83, l. 7	749	784
p. 103, n. 83, l. 8	784	749
p. 104, l. 1	Jacopo di Guiccardini	Jacopo Guicciardini
p. 104, n. 86	institutit	instituit
p. 106, l. 22	Malatesta Novella	Malatesta Novello
p. 106, n. 94, l. 3	aluunt	alunt
p. 110, n. 107	(quicquid)	quicquam esse
p. 111, n. 108, l. 1	adunantem	abundantem
p. 113, l. 7	Panormità	Panormita
p. 114, l. 19	Antonio Panormità	Antonio Beccadelli, il Panormita
p. 126, l. 1	Burgo Campi	Borgo del Campo
p. 134, n. 56, l. 2	patitus	patitur
p. 136, l. 11	new tables of proscriptions,	confiscations, proscriptions,
p. 136, n. 66, l. 4	tabulae novae proscriptiones,	tabulae novae, proscriptiones,
p. 137, n. 74	aerumnias	aerumnas
p. 137, n. 75, l. 4	sperebam	sperabam
p. 138, n. 76, l. 3	ad hinc	ab hinc
p. 139, l. 11	Carpo	Carpi

PREFACE

THE following pages investigate the character and cultural significance of the attitude towards happiness of the Italian humanists. The persons here selected as representatives of humanism are Italian writers from the fourteenth to the sixteenth century who have usually been so regarded. The intensity of their fidelity to classical and renaissance ideals, however, varied greatly, and any such generic designation of a group of writers as humanists is necessarily loose and approximate. Since humanism was by definition professedly more concerned with human interests and problems, especially as these were reflected in non-Christian classical literature, the subject of the individual's happiness, it has been assumed, was its peculiar concern to a far greater extent than in earlier Christian medieval thought and writing. The validity of the assumption will be tested in an exposition of humanist writings on happiness and in a comparison of them with certain standard Christian medieval considerations of the same topic.

Specifically, the writings of humanism on *Happiness, True Nobility, Human Dignity* and related themes—all of which centered about the definition of the *summum bonum* and its usual identification with happiness—will be considered. In addition, certain discussions of the effect of *Calamities* and other disturbances of man's internal composure by the exterior world contribute to an understanding of the humanists' attitudes. With some exceptions, treatment will be restricted to works of this nature—i.e. writings bearing directly on the problem of individual happiness.

Although the scope is necessarily limited by the availability of the works, it is hoped that the selection which has been made because of this restriction will not result in an entirely unrepresentative picture of humanism. The humanists also composed treatises on other subjects that might seem relevant to the question of happiness but have been excluded from systematic consideration. Such a theme was *Fortune*. The litera-

5

ture on this topic will not be discussed specifically because *Fortune* was regarded as only one of the possible goods in which *Happiness* might be found. Its role, therefore, had anyhow to be assayed in considering works on the individual's pursuit of happiness. The value of goods of fortune are quite adequately evaluated by the humanists in the literature here covered. It will also be treated in connection with the works on *Calamities*. A survey of humanist literature on *Fortune* may be found in the studies made by Howard R. Patch and by Alfred Doren.[1]

Thanks are due to many persons who have been of assistance and encouragement in preparing this study. Not of least aid have been the librarians of the Library of Columbia University, of the Chapin Library of Williams College, of the Widener Library of Harvard College, of the New York Public Library, of the British Museum and of the Bibliothèque Nationale. I am indebted to my colleagues Dr. Henry A. Ladd and Dr. Helen N. McMaster of Sarah Lawrence College, to Professor Alice D. Snyder of Vassar College, to Professors Salo Baron, Austin P. Evans, Jefferson B. Fletcher and John H. Randall, Jr. of Columbia University for many valuable suggestions improving the manuscript. Of Professor Lynn Thorndike, under whose direction I have worked, I can only state that without the initial training in this field which I received from him, without the patience and understanding with which he kept me working within reasonable and practicable bounds, this study could never have existed.

1 Howard Rollin Patch, "The Tradition of the Goddess Fortuna in Medieval Philosophy and Literature", pp. 179-235, *Smith College Studies in Modern Languages*, vol. III, Northampton, 1922, especially chap. IV, "Fortune in Italian Literature from Dante to the Renaissance", pp. 204-230. Alfred Doren, "Fortuna im Mittelalter und in der Renaissance", pp. 71-144, *Vorträge der Bibliothek Warburg,* Teil I, Hamburg, 1922-23.

TABLE OF CONTENTS

CHAPTER I

THE HAPPY HUMANIST, A
MODERN CREATION

IT is a common opinion that the self-seeking and individual-istic man believes that his egoism can make him happy. This belief was projected into the Renaissance, and, as a result, it has been widely held that because the humanists were vain and greedy self-seekers they also favored the modern view that the pursuit of personal utility made for happiness. As a corollary to this doctrine, it has been thought that the humanists considered both human capacities and the world in which they lived well adapted to yielding happiness to whosoever pursued it.

Supposedly the classical source for this opinion was Jacob Burckhardt. An important influence on the teachings of Nietzsche, Burckhardt revealed in his famous work, *The Civilization of the Renaissance in Italy*,[1] a frank admiration for the men of a time that made personal power, wealth or fame the goal in life; he reiterated the slogan of Michelet, " The Discovery of Man and the World." Yet even Burckhardt was forced to make some reservations in this conception of the period. His only outspoken statement implying optimism —" The Renaissance prevailed in times and cities where the tendency was to enjoy life heartily "—was relegated to a foot-note.[2] Even this statement was modified by adding a sentence setting a temporal limit to this acceptance of the goodness of life. " The general darkening of the spirit of thoughtful men did not begin to show itself till the time of the foreign supremacy in the sixteenth century." In one place he spoke openly of the pessimism of the humanists. " With respect to the moral

1 *Die Cultur der Renaissance in Italien.* Zweite durchgesehene Auflage, Leipzig, 1869, References will also be to the Fourth Edition of the English translation by S. G. C. Middlemore, London, 1898.

2 *Ibid.,* German, p. 365, n. 1; trans., p. 456, n. 1.

government of the world, the humanists seldom get beyond a cold and resigned consideration of the prevalent violence and misrule. . . Distinguished men drew up a debit and credit of the happiness and unhappiness of their lives, and generally found that the latter outweighed the former." [3]

Perhaps the impression that Burckhardt was the great proponent of the view that an affirmative doctrine of individualism first became an important element in European consciousness with the Italian humanists has been derived rather more from the enthusiastic tone of his delineation of the men of that period than from specific pleading on his part. He tried to show how, for many humanists, the fame of a great achievement or a spectacular career became a goal of life. A distinct personality setting one man off from another was sought after in one's own life and noticed in the lives of others. Psychological analysis was a favorite theme of poetry; biographical literature abounded; physical beauty, especially feminine, was an object of admiration; and particular modes of life, such as the rustic, were vividly described. [4]

3 *Ibid.*, German, p. 407; trans., p. 503.

4 *Ibid.*, particularly Part II, "The Development of the Individual," and Part IV, "The Discovery of the World and of Man." The following citations are some random selections of Burckhardt's expressions of enthusiasm and gratuitous praise for the men of this period:

German, p. 225; trans., p. 289; after referring to Gerbert and Roger Bacon as men of science in spite of their times, "It is another matter when a whole people takes a natural delight in the study and investigation of nature, at a time when other nations are indifferent—that is to say, when the discoverer is not threatened or wholly ignored, but can count on the friendly support of congenial spirits. That this was the case in Italy is unquestionable."

German, p. 241; trans., p. 308; "This period, as we have seen, first gave the highest development to individuality, and then led the individual to the most zealous and thorough study of himself in all forms and under all conditions."

German, p. 261; trans., p. 329; after claiming that the Middle Ages had no sense of personality, "Among the Italians, on the contrary, the search for the characteristic features of remarkable men was a prevailing tendency; and this it is which separates them from other Western peoples, among whom the same thing happens but seldom, and in exceptional cases. This

Here it may be noted that these conclusions were based for the most part on the polite literature. The only work of theoretical pretensions cited was Giovanni Pico's *The Dignity of Man*.[5]

It is in just this neglected area of formal and systematic treatments of the nature of happiness and the means of attaining it that this study is going to venture. And in it two of Burckhardt's theses will be submitted to examination: first, that the nature of the humanists' interest, in keeping with the social life of the times, was individualistic and psychological, and secondly, that because of this concern with their personal experience of life the humanists showed enthusiasm for the good things of this world. It will come out below that the second assumption is gratuitous, since the intensity of the pursuit of personal happiness may equally well or even with greater justice be a function of the acuteness of personal misery than an indication of genial approval of man and the world.

Burckhardt also tried to show that the humanists had a deep appreciation of the beauties of nature and were interested in the world about them both in its remote geography and in the intimate details of their native cities. He did not fail to add his own word of caution. " The facts which we shall quote

keen eye for individuality belongs only to those who have emerged from the half-conscious life of the race and become themselves individuals."

German, p. 269; trans., p. 338; " But from the first the Italians surpassed all others in their quick apprehension of the mental differences among cities and populations."

German, p. 271; trans., p. 343; " On reading the Italian authors of that period attentively we are astounded at the keenness and accuracy with which outward features are seized, and at the completeness with which personal appearance in general is described."

German, p. 276; trans., p. 348; " The comical and satirical literature of the Middle Ages could not dispense with pictures of everyday events. But it is another thing when the Italians of the Renaissance dwelt on this picture for its own sake—for its inherent interest—and because it forms part of that great universal life of the world whose magic breath they felt everywhere around them."

5 *Ibid.*, German, pp. 281-82; trans., p. 354; See below, pp. 66-7, 100 for discussions of this treatise.

in evidence of our thesis will be few in number . . . the author is conscious that he is treading on the perilous ground of conjecture. . ." [6]

All of this seems at first glance to be evidence of a favorable estimation of life in this world and of human nature. With the possible exceptions of the idealization of the life of rustics and the pursuit of natural beauty, both of which attitudes might also be interpreted as implying a condemnation of the turmoil of urban life and a desire to escape from it,[7] these attitudes, culled from the literature by Burckhardt, in some instances probably do indicate an enthusiastic quest for advantage and a virile egoism.

In addition to the strictures that can be placed on Burckhardt's interpretation because of his neglect of the evidence of theoretical discussions of mundane and human worth, his estimate of the life of the period is still further limited in its significance by the failure to consider that similar enthusiasm for life and egoistic modes of behavior have characterized in part many other historical periods, notably the Middle Ages. It may be that life was lived differently in the cities of Italy in the time of the humanists, but in what way it is hard to tell from Burckhardt's description.

Burckhardt added another side to his own picture when he discussed " Morality and Religion " in Part IV. He cited humanists railing against the moral degeneracy and weakness of men of their time. He was shocked himself by the sordid pictures of crime and of the depths of human decay he was able to draw out of the contemporary histories. Men of all sorts sought solace from the terrors, violence, uncertainty, and inanity of life in great religious movements. The reforming preacher was never more popular. Other men sought to avert

6 Burckhardt, *op. cit.*, German, pp. 241-42; trans., p. 308.

7 For example, in the case of Petrarch, *De Vita Solitaria,* Eng. trans. by Jacob Zeitlin, Urbana, 1924, from which Burckhardt quotes glowing descriptions of natural loveliness, a profound disillusionment with the chaotic flux of fortune in the city is also present.

disasters or to mollify the consequences of calamities by recourse to the stars, to sorcery, to fatalistic doctrines of many kinds. Bold and free thinkers experienced conversions, or revealed their lack of confidence in their own powers to cope with the world by yielding to this or that superstition. Conditions could not have been propitious for the achievement of the personal happiness which was sought.

Burckhardt, however, looked upon the darker side of his picture as revealing a severe and undisciplined form of the individualism he so admired. Or else these reactions were the heroic remedies needed to temper the prevalent extremes of individualism. More serious than this inclination to reconcile contradictory motifs in the activities of the time under the broad rubric of individualism was Burckhardt's failure to give full consideration to the theoretical works of the humanists. He assumed that the practical philosophy of the period was worldly and egoistic, and that it necessarily conflicted with Christian theology and the moral standards of the Church. It did not occur to him that the life men lived might also have come into conflict with what they felt about life, feelings which might often be more in harmony with the teachings of the Church than with the practical activities of the times.

Since Burckhardt such a unified, well-rounded view of the culture of the period has been abandoned by many historians. They have sought to give different interpretations. Nevertheless, they too have often succumbed to the intriguing possibilities of finding some principle of unity between theory and practice. For them too the question of how so much antagonism to a lusty, worldly existence could possibly be present in the thought of the humanists, when the time in which they lived provided plentiful examples of boisterous, or calculated pursuit of wealth and pleasure, has remained a stumbling block.

Heinrich Thode felt that " the movement of humanity " was an expression of the personal, subjective kind of religious feeling which had grown out of St. Francis' reconciliation of the worldliness and egoism of the townsmen, unrealizable as long

as the authority of the Church survived, with the otherworldliness and universality of the Church. The spiritual striving for
individualism could not be gratified within the bounds of the
old social organization, so that it had to be delimited, turned
inward and brought under the control of the Church. The confident pursuit of personal gain on the part of the citizens had
to be reconciled with the opposing theories of the Church. St.
Francis " led the progressive, impetuous torrent into the delimited channel and thus earned the eternal merit of having
preserved it against an untimely dispersion, assembled its
powers and directed it toward a single goal. The goal is the
introversion of men, the blissful, restricted bed of Christian
theory . . ." [8] The outcome of the Franciscan mediating
influence was not unrestricted individualism but rather dis-
ciplined spiritual submission to authority. Thode saw the humanist movement as a part of a general movement toward individualism and inner worldliness culminating in the Protestant
Reformation. Since his time it has been made clear how little
logical or historical connection there was between the culture
of the humanists of fifteenth century Italy and the religious
upheavals of the sixteenth century beyond the Alps. [9] Nevertheless, Thode's efforts were significant because they first called
attention to the religious and otherworldly aspects of the humanists' thought, which had been overlooked by Burckhardt.

Following the lead of Thode, Alfred von Martin sought to
show the analogies between the humanist and the monastic or
mendicant ideals of life as illustrated in the writings of
Coluccio Salutati. In spite of the mockery and derision of
monks and mendicants by certain humanists, there was much
in the humanist ideal of life that was analogous to Christian
asceticism. Virtue was regarded as the true end of man and
was defined as knowledge or science. The virtuous or wise man

8 Heinrich Thode, *Franz von Assisi und die Anfänge der Kunst der
Renaissance in Italien,* 2nd ed., Berlin, 1904, " Einleitung," p. xxiv.

9 By Ernst Troeltsch, for example, " Renaissance und Reformation,"
Gesammelte Schriften, Tübingen, 1923, vol. IV, pp. 270 ff.

gave up worldly pursuits and the sensual pleasures for study and virtue.[10]

Ernst Cassirer believed that the apparent opposition between the preaching and the practice of the humanists could be resolved in another way. The humanists differed from the scholastics mainly on the question of style. Indeed, " the philosophy of the Quattrocento was and remained, even in its most significant and consequential directions, theology." [11] This seeming opposition between the systematic thought and the apparently worldly pursuits of the humanists had led Burckhardt, in his efforts to achieve a comprehensive view of the period, to neglect the philosophy.[12] By attempting to find certain key problems common to all writers amid the welter of conflicting tendencies, Cassirer hoped that " the question of the relationship in which theoretical intellectual activity stood to the other forces of life . . . would then be answered by itself." [13] The problem which, he thought, concerned all writers was the relationship of the individual to the universe, and the solution to which all writers tended was the discovery of subjective self-consciousness, which gave the individual power to control his own destiny. Writers ceased to be satisfied with the belief that the destiny of one's own soul and existence was to be found in submission to the grace of a transcendent deity. Instead they began to find it in the divinity immanent within man. In the fifteenth century Cassirer believed that Marsilio Ficino and Giovanni Pico best exemplified this attitude. The way was thus prepared for the more clearly subjective, idealistic philosophy of Descartes and Leibniz.[14]

10 Alfred von Martin, *Coluccio Salutati und das Humanistische Lebensideal*, comprising Band 23 of *Beiträge zur Kulturgeschichte des Mittelalters und der Renaissance*, Leipzig and Berlin, 1916, pp. 93-95. Cited hereafter as von Martin, I. See below, pp. 57-63 for further discussion of von Martin.

11 Ernst Cassirer, *Individuum und Kosmos in der Philosophie der Renaissance, Studien der Bibliothek Warburg*, X, Leipzig and Berlin, 1927, p. 4.

12 *Ibid.*, pp. 3-4.   13 *Ibid.*, p. 6.

14 *Ibid.*, especially Kap. 4, " Das Subjekt-Objekt-Problem in der Philosophie der Renaissance," pp. 130-31.

Even Cassirer, with his idealistic tendency to regard the empirical success of modern science in conquering nature and in reducing the hazards of earthly existence as growing out of metaphysical speculation,[15] was forced to admit that humanist thought did not always portray man as having a confident and favorable adjustment with his world. " Thus a thoroughly one-sided picture of the disposition of life of the Florentine circle will be gained, if one wishes to judge it mainly after the hymns of Lorenzo the Magnificent." The rapid turning to Savonarola was understandable " only if the ascetic propensities are considered which from the beginning were mixed in their view of the world." These tendencies were evident in the writings of Ficino and Giovanni Pico.

In a recent study partially reviving Thode's thesis, Hans Baron has tried to show that until the fifteenth century Italian humanists shared the mendicants' views that wealth was valueless. " Of the complex world of antiquity, they [the early humanists] recognized only the features akin to the pessimism and renunciation of life which took possession of mankind in the period following the terrible epidemics in the middle of the fourteenth century. Seldom in the course of the Middle Ages has so much been written concerning the ' miseria ' of human beings and human life as here at its end, and it was particularly the advocates of Petrarch's humanism who contributed to this literature." [16]

Baron eliminated the question of a conflict between the theory and practice of the fourteenth century humanists by assuming that, since they were for the most part poor,

15 This well known thesis, set forth in E. A. Burtt, *The Metaphysical Foundations of Modern Physical Science*, New York, 1925, on the inspiration of Cassirer's views, has been recently criticized in E. W. Strong, *Procedures and Metaphysics*, Berkeley, 1936. Strong shows the lack of connection between the Neoplatonic humanists and the later scientists, the wide divergence of the interests and problems of the two groups, the growth of metaphysics after the scientific discoveries as a working out of their implications.

16 Hans Baron, " Franciscan Poverty and Civic Wealth as Factors in the Rise of Humanistic Thought," *Speculum*, XIII, 1, January 1938, p. 12.

wandering scholars and secretaries, there was no real conflict between their doctrines and their activities.[17] In the fifteenth century, however, a conflict developed when wealthy citizens began to participate in intellectual life.[18] But the gap was soon closed by a shift on the part of the humanists from a doctrine of poverty to an affirmation of the place of wealth and worldly activity in life.[19] Baron, however, did not really solve the problem of the contradiction of thought and action for more than a few humanists. He recognized that this-worldliness was limited mainly to certain Florentine writers of the first half of the fifteenth century and that hostility to worldliness was revived by others.[20]

This study has grown out of and is built upon previous considerations of the ethical teachings of the humanists. It differs from them in rejecting the belief, enunciated at the beginning of this chapter, that feelings of personal satisfaction and the corresponding doctrine of worldliness must accompany a life-pattern of pursuit of self-interest and material gain. This is an assumption which is false, or, at the very most, limited to special circumstances. That the facts of the renaissance period do not warrant this belief, the difficulties of historians would seem to indicate. To deny the universality of the assumption which has been characteristic of previous efforts in this field is not to deny that there is a relationship of some kind between external behavior and inner feelings and theoretical ideals. Individual life and culture are frequently complex so that differing trends and many variations among them may legitimately be expected.

Both ethical individualism in the doctrine that self-interest and personal utility are the measures of all value and the altruistic admonition to subordinate private advantage to the interests of others or of some higher ideal (God, the State, the

17 *Ibid.*, p. 12.
18 *Ibid.*, p. 18.
19 *Ibid.*, pp. 18 ff.
20 *Ibid.*, pp. 26 and especially 31 ff.

Social Order, Morality) have been characteristic modern attitudes. It seems strange that historians, moved by the zeal to
make moderns of the humanists, should have sought to fit
them into only one of the moulds. It was probably not an accident that Burckhardt, who created the pattern for many interpretations of the Renaissance, should have emphasized the
egoistic trends of the period. It is significant that his book
influenced Nietzsche's affirmation of the dynamic power of the
individual.

It is unnecessary to assume that doctrinal egoism and altruism are diametrically opposed theories. It is merely necessary to
recognize that pursuit of self-interest in practice was apt to
give rise to a condition of insecurity—the " variety " and the
" uncertainty " of the humanists—which in some cases would
have as its theoretical result altruism, anti-worldliness, resignation or despair. In other individuals of stouter character the
condition of insecurity might not have influenced their thought
and the doctrine proclaimed that happiness consisted in the
achievement of individual rewards of a material nature. The
entire political and economic development of late medieval Italy
compelled an ever-widening circle of persons to engage in a
mutually competitive struggle for self-advancement. The very
conditions of that competition, whatever the field of activity,
jeopardized the possession of any gains made in it and thus
rendered happiness or even satisfaction in the personal goods
achieved precarious. In this situation the humanists were at a
peculiar disadvantage. Conceiving matters in this fashion, is
it so difficult to account for the fact that the humanists, indeed,
seemed to pursue the advantages of this world, while many of
them believed that happiness had to be found in a variety of
other, usually self-denying, ways?

CHAPTER II

THE MEDIEVAL CHRISTIAN VIEW
OF HAPPINESS

ANOTHER modern assumption in need of examination is the view that the teachings of medieval Catholicism were characterized by a much lower estimate of the happiness of human life on earth than certain modern idealistic and materialistic philosophies. It will be interesting to see how the doctrines of some medieval writers compare with the humanists' theories. Strictly speaking, the position of the Church cannot be said to have altogether condemned worldly values as a means toward happiness. The world and human nature were not held to be evil of themselves but merely relatively evil when contrasted with the greater good of the other world and especially with the absolute goodness of God. Goodness was seen in the world and in man's earthly state, but not goodness in its very essence, rather goodness as it served as a means to a divine purpose. Prior to the Fall the goodness of man and the world had been unlimited. After the Fall they had become corrupted; man by willing and exercising his faculty of intelligence could regain goodness through the mediation of divine grace. Thus the Church did not regard this life as either evil in very essence or by nature perfectly good; it held a compromise position judging man and the world according to given situations.[1]

1 Ernst Troeltsch, *Die Soziallehren der christlichen Kirchen und Gruppen, Gesammelte Schriften,* Band I, 3d ed., Tübingen, 1923, p. 103, n. 52, in reference to the limited character of asceticism in Christian doctrine cites Augustine's distinction between *frui* and *uti* with regard to worldly goods. "It is not asceticism in the proper sense, but the nullification of the value in themselves of all goods of this world. But therein asceticism properly so-called was easily inserted—the mortification of nature and the denial of the natural will. The entire early Christian and medieval position on the world moved back and forth between the two thoughts, a clear indication that not asceticism but otherworldliness—the setting of a specific, religious life-purpose above all worldly interests in the holy community—is its more

Within this doctrine, which neither rejected nor affirmed life in this world, it was not difficult for the Church to lean to one side or the other in emphasis. Some theologians tended toward semi-Pelagian or crypto-semi-Pelagian positions which, if carried too far, were heretical in optimistically overemphasizing the favorable aspects of worldly life.[2] Other writers, especially those making a special plea for asceticism, veered toward the pessimistic heresies of Gnosticism or Manicheanism.[3] Within the boundaries separating orthodoxy from these two heresies a writer might appear optimistic or pessimistic, as he leaned to one side or the other, emphasizing the potentiality for good in the world or man, or contrasting the corrupting passions of the flesh and the passing pleasures of this life with the eternal bliss of the next.

The view, which even today occasionally manifests itself, that the writers of the Middle Ages or of the Church were inclined to belittle human values and condemn this life, was probably based on a one-sided reading of only those works which reveal such an attitude. The classic of this type of literature was Innocent III's *Contempt for the World or the Misery of Human Condition*.[4] It would be a mistake to use this treatise as an examplar of the medieval view of happiness. Indeed, In-

essential, basic idea. Asceticism first exerted power as a means to protection against the over-strong competition of worldly purposes and more surely achieved the goal through entirely denying the earthly rather than merely limiting it . . . Therewith, to be sure, asceticism often enough grew to be an end in itself, but where this was strictly the case, it also always ran near a byway into radical monasticism, strange to the Christian idea and suspicious to the Church, or into pantheistic mysticism. It is thoroughly logical if the Church has always guarded itself further against this byway."
Adolf Harnack, *Lehrbuch der Dogmengeschichte*, Freiburg i. B., 1890, Band 3, pp. 82-3, speaks similarly of the two directions of thought in St. Augustine.

2 Friederich Loofs, *Leitfaden zum Studium der Dogmengeschichte*, 4th ed., Halle, 1906, pp. 544-49, treats Alexander of Hales and Bonaventura and Albertus Magnus as neo-semi-Pelagians.

3 *Cf.* passage cited from Troeltsch in n. 1.

4 *De Contemptu Mundi seu de Miseria Humanae Conditionis Libri Tres*, in J. P. Migne, *Patrologia Latina*, T. 217, cols. 701-746, Paris, 1855.

nocent, himself, recognized that the work represented but an extremity of mood of only one side of the entire medieval position. In his opening dedication he refers to the opposite theme of the *Dignity and Excellence of Man* and promises to write on it sometime in the future.[5]

An equally distorted view of the Renaissance is gained if the treatises on the happier view of man are taken alone. Some of these treatises will be considered in the following chapter, and it is noteworthy that in one case the humanist Bartolomeo Fazio begins his discussion of man's excellence by remarking that he is carrying out the promise Innocent III failed to fulfill.[6] In addition Gianozzo Manetti devoted a long passage to taking up Innocent's assertions one by one and stating the converse.[7] This is another reason why Innocent need not be considered at this point.

St. Augustine (354-430), Petrarch's imaginary guide and counselor, aptly illustrates the tendency of orthodox writers before the time of the humanists to emphasize both the misery and evil of life in this world and the possibilities for happiness and good therein. As will emerge, Augustine approached the problem of happiness from a psychological point of view such as marked the attitude of many humanists. In this way he focussed the discussion directly on the plight of the individual. In addition he attempted to expound and refute the philosophic positions of the Stoics, the Aristotelians, the Platonists and the Epicureans, all of whom found their representatives among the humanists. Many of his passages, both those taking a negative and those taking a positive attitude toward human life, became literary models for future discussions. As orthodox as the position of St. Thomas, Augustine's attitude in contrast more nearly approached the mood with which the humanists, even those who differed in their solutions, embarked upon a discussion of happiness.

5 *Ibid.*, col. 701.
6 See below, p. 73.
7 See below, pp. 72-76.

He treated the question in the famous 19th book of the *City of God,* where he shows the superiority of Christianity in bringing a release from earthly sorrows over the false escapes of the pagan philosophies.[8] This discussion is supplemented by the 22nd book which deals with the joys of eternal, heavenly life after the resurrection and contrasts them with the miseries of earthly existence. Chapter 24 of this book, however, deals with the favorable side of this life in such glowing terms that, if it were taken out of its context, Augustine would deserve recognition as one of the world's greatest optimists. The contrast between the two attitudes could not be sharper, or better adapted to demonstrating the opposing optimistic and pessimistic tendencies existing side by side within orthodox Christianity.

Book 19 is worth discussing in some detail, since it takes up the problems of the misery of human conditions, happiness, and the *summum bonum,* which were favorite topics of the humanists. Chapters, 1, 2, and 3 take up " the reasonings by which men have attempted to make for themselves a happiness in this unhappy life " as outlined by Marcus Varro in *De Philosophia,* a work that is no longer extant. The usual definition of happiness as consisting in the supreme good and the definition of this as " that for the sake of which other things are to be desired, while it is to be desired for its own sake " are given.[9] Varro's argument is then outlined. Men by nature desire four things: pleasure (sensual), repose (freedom from discomfort), the two combined (called pleasure by Epicurus) and the primary objects of nature (including the first three and health, intelligence, etc.). Virtue is also desired in some combination with these, but desire for it is acquired through instruction rather than through nature. Hypothetically there can be 288 philosophical sects. According as each of the four

8 Augustinus Aurelius, *De Civitate Dei Libri XXII,* English translation by Marcus Dods, ed. by Philip Schaff, *A Select Library of the Nicene and Post-Nicene Fathers of the Christian Church,* Buffalo, 1887, vol. II.

9 *Ibid.,* p. 397.

natural desires is made the means, the end or the equal of virtue, twelve sects result. These ends may be desired for one-self or socially for friends, making twenty-four. They may be held as certain or only probable making forty-eight. The Cynic dress may or may not be adopted making ninety-six. They may involve a contemplative life, an active life or a balance of both making 288 sects in all. But all these factors which multiply the sects involve no difference over the supreme good, and the sects can be reduced to the four natural desires combined in three ways with virtue making twelve. But since the first three nat-ural desires are included under the fourth—primary objects of nature—the sects are reduced to three: that which holds that the primary objects of nature are to be desired for virtue's sake, that which holds virtue is to be desired for their sake, and that which holds that virtue and these objects are to be desired each for its own sake. The supreme good of man is in question, and man is made of body and soul, neither one nor the other alone, but both together. Therefore both primary ob-jects and virtue are desired, one for the body and the other for the soul, but virtue is the greater. The happy life is social, knowledge of it is certain, dress is indifferent, and the com-posite is the better mode.[10] This is the position of the old Academy, according to Varro, and, as will be seen, the position of the Aristotelians according to Leonardo Bruni, who favored it.[11]

For Augustine, however, " life eternal is the supreme good, death eternal the supreme evil." Varro's position, as well as the others, is judged to be this-worldly and optimistic. " As for those who have supposed that the sovereign good and evil are to be found in this life, and have placed it either in the soul or the body, or in both . . . all these have, with a marvellous shal-lowness, sought to find their blessedness in this life and in themselves." There follows a vivid passage, bitterly denouncing the false hope of happiness in this life. " For what flood of

10 *Ibid.,* Chapters 1, 2, 3, pp. 397-401.
11 See below, pp. 109-112.

eloquence can suffice to detail the miseries of this life? . . . For when, where, how in this life can these primary objects of nature be possessed so that they may not be assailed by unforeseen accidents?" The body can not be free from pain when decay, deformity, weakness, lassitude, and sluggishness attack it. Many things destroy bodily beauty and grace. The senses are attacked by blindness, deafness, and disease. Delirium ends intellect. Demons possess men.[12] Virtue, because it has to wage perpetual war against vices, means suffering and labor. We cannot keep the flesh from warring against the spirit. "Far be it from us, then, to fancy that, while we are still engaged in this intestine war, we have already found the happiness which we wish to seek by victory." Prudence, justice and fortitude mean constant misery and turmoil.[13]

At this point the pagan philosophies are taken up and shown to be fallacious. "And I am at a loss to understand how the Stoic philosophers can presume to say that these [bodily and earthly sufferings] are no ills, though at the same time they allow the wise man to commit suicide and to pass out of this life, if it becomes so grievous that he cannot or ought not to endure it. But such is the stupid pride of these men who fancy that the supreme good can be found in this life, and that they can become happy by their resources, that their wise man, or at least the man whom they fancifully depict as such, is always happy, even though he become blind, deaf, dumb, mutilated, wracked with pains, or suffer any conceivable calamity such as may compel him to make away with himself: and they are not ashamed to call the life that is beset with evils happy. O happy life, which seeks the aid of death to end it!"[14] It must be said on behalf of the Stoics, however, that their estimate of life in this world was by no means as bright as Augustine charges, for happiness was achieved only by the conquest of fear and desire through prudence, fortitude and the other

12 *Ibid.*, p. 401.
13 *Ibid.*, p. 402.
14 *Idem.*

moral virtues according to the Stoics. Augustine would have agreed to this if he had thought such a conquest possible; for him it could be achieved only by the aid of the divine grace. The Stoics felt that it could not be achieved with any ease, but considered it possible for a very few men—as rare as the phoenix, as they put it—to achieve happiness by means of their own powers.[15]

Similarly, " Those who admit that these are evils, as the Peripatetics do, and the Old Academy, the sect which Varro advocates, express a more intelligible doctrine; but theirs also is a surprising mistake, for they contend that this is a happy life which is beset by these evils, even though they be so great that he who endures them should commit suicide to escape them." [16] The Aristotelians and the Platonists, who saw good in bodily well-being and conceded greater possibility for gaining happiness through the things of this world than Augustine did, were, indeed, more optimistic than the Christians, who saw no good in worldly possessions and physical comfort as such. Yet Augustine's dark view of this life was otherworldly rather than ascetic, for it admitted that suffering and material hardship were evil. In this way he came closer to these philosophers than to the Stoics, who admitted that suffering was an evil only when one was not strong-willed enough to become indifferent to it. On the other hand, the Stoics in their view that material prosperity did not confer happiness were closer to Augustine than the others. All three were pessimistic so far as the chances of happiness in this world were concerned, for, aside from their disagreement about what the greatest good might be, all approximated each other in feeling that material and psychological security were either extremely difficult or impossible to gain. In this respect the Christian tended to be a little more realistic than the others.

But in another sense Augustine was more optimistic than any, for he could look forward to happiness in the world to

15 Edwyn Bevan, *Stoics and Sceptics,* Oxford, 1913, p. 71.
16 *Op. cit.,* p. 403.

come, and this very hope would give him strength to endure the pains of this world. " This life, then, which is either subject to accidents, or environed with evils so considerable and grievous, could never have been called happy, if the men who gave it this name . . . had not fancied that the supreme good was to be found in this mortal life. . . By the hope of the future world, this life, which is miserably involved in the many and great evils of this world, is happy as it is also safe. . . And this happiness these philosophers refuse to believe in, because they do not see it, and attempt to fabricate for themselves a happiness in this life, based upon a virtue which is as deceitful as it is proud." [17]

The succeeding chapters take up the misery involved in family life, in cities, in relations with other nations, in friendship with men, in friendship with angels (for demons frequently and deceitfully pose as angels).[18]

Augustine returns to the same theme in Book 22, where, after discussing the nature of heavenly life, he affirms, Chapter 22, " that the whole human race has been condemned in its first origin," to which " this life itself, if life it is to be called, bears witness by the host of cruel ills with which it is filled." [19] This is proved by the multitude of errors produced by man's ignorance, " by his love of so many vain hurtful things, which produce gnawing cares, . . . [he lists forty-eight different humans ills]." [20] The human error which produces them is present from infancy, but God's mercy has provided law and education to help overcome them; these institutions, however, " are themselves full of labor and sorrow." " But besides the punishments of childhood, without which there would be no learning of what the parents wish—and the parents rarely wish anything useful to be taught—who can describe, who can conceive the number and severity of the punishments which afflict the human

17 *Idem.*
18 *Ibid.,* Chapters 5-9, pp. 403-06.
19 *Ibid.,* p. 499.
20 *Ibid.,* pp. 499-500.

race,—pains which are not only the accompaniment of the wickedness of godless men, but are part of the human condition and the common misery . . . ? " [21] Even the good are subject to " the crimes and wicked deeds of other men." All men suffer robbery, captivity, chains, prison, exile, torture, mutilation, loss of sight, violation of chastity, extremes of heat and cold, floods, lightning, thunder, hail, earthquakes, houses falling, stumbling horses, poisons from fruits, air, water, animals, bites of mad dogs, shipwreck, domestic accidents, destruction of crops, assaults of demons, bodily diseases, pangs of thirst and hunger leading to cannibalism, nightmares. Only through divine grace is some consolation afforded. Even the pagans admitted that very few men have received the divine gift of the power to withstand calamity.[22]

Chapter 24—" Of the Blessings with which the Creator Has Filled this Life, Obnoxious though it be to the Curse "—is in most striking contrast to the dismal picture preceding. (Chapter 23 adds more on the miseries which even the righteous suffer in trying to combat evil.) Since God created the world, the world cannot be an evil place, for that would make God, whose essential nature is goodness, the producer of evil. On the other hand, God cannot be conceived as struggling against an original evil power or evil state of formlessness, for that would deprive God of his power as Creator and lead to dualism. On these logical grounds Christian thought has always had a difficult time with the problems of earthly evil and goodness.[23] Augustine's solution of the dilemma was to introduce evil into the world through man's original sin, which God countered with punishment. In condemning human nature, " He did not withdraw all that He had given it, else it had been annihilated."

21 *Ibid.*, p. 500.

22 *Ibid.*, pp. 500-01.

23 For histories of these problems from the metaphysical point of view, J. Boodin, *Three Interpretations of the Universe*, New York, 1934; from the doctrinal point of view, K. E. Kirk, *The Vision of God, the Christian Doctrine of the Summum Bonum*, Bampton Lectures for 1928, London, 1931.

God did not remove evil from His power but placed it under His control. The presence of partial good in the world is necessary for the continuity of the work of creation. Thus although man became mortal, he retained the power of propagation, degraded, as it was, to the bestial level. Propagation is a creative power which God originally conferred upon man as a blessing of good. Along with it He conferred another power— that of conformation. In man's fallen state, man generates man not through his own power, but only through God's creative power of conformation. Thus the species is continued. The partial goodness left by God in this world is a goodness by virtue of being a continuation of the creation. This continuing creative activity of God " causes the seed to develop, and to evolve from certain secret folds into the visible forms of beauty which we see." [24]

God, in this way, gave a mind with the capacities of reason and understanding to the human soul. With these the soul acquires wisdom and arms itself with the virtues of prudence, fortitude, temperance and righteousness by which it can struggle against error and vice " by fixing its desires upon no other object than the supreme and unchangeable Good." [25] Besides this power, there are the countless arts invented by man through necessity or exuberance, which, although given to the superfluous, dangerous and destructive, still bring many useful things. " What wonderful . . . advantage has human industry made in the arts of weaving and building, of agriculture and navigation! With what endless variety are designs in pottery, painting, and sculpture produced, and with what skill executed! What wonderful spectacles are exhibited in the theatres . . . How skillful the contrivances for catching, killing, or taming wild beasts! . . . Who could tell the thought that has been spent on nature. . .?" [26] No modern apostle of progress could be more eloquent in extolling the powers of man over his environ-

24 *Op. cit.*, p. 502.
25 *Ibid.*, p. 503.
26 *Idem.*

ment than Augustine in this passage. But it is easy to forget that this is only one side of the picture he gives and not the most frequent side. Indeed, Augustine hastened to retract its significance for glorifying man by pointing out the moral that the nature of the human mind, great as it is, " could never have fallen into these miseries, nor have gone out of them to miseries eternal — saving only those who are redeemed — had not an exceeding great sin been found in the first man from whom the rest have sprung." [27]

Even though the human body dies like that of beasts and is weaker, the goodness of God is apparent in it. The organs of sense, the limbs, the form and stature of the body are shaped for the use of the soul. " Man has not been created stooping towards the earth like the irrational animals; but his bodily form, erect and looking heavenwards, admonishes him to mind the things that are above." [28] The tongue and hands are well adapted to many duties and arts, and all parts combine utility and beauty. The dissections of the anatomists have been unable to discover the secret of bodily harmony. Some bodily parts are designed only for beauty and not for utility, while all are beautiful, so that the body is meant more for comeliness than necessity.[29]

" How can I tell of the rest of the creation, with all its beauty and utility . . .? Shall I speak of the manifold and various loveliness of sky, and earth, and sea; . . . of the shade of trees; of the colors and perfume of flowers; . . .? " There are the different kinds of foods, the art of cookery, the alternation of night and day, the clothing supplied from plants and animals. " Who can enumerate all the blessings we enjoy? . . . And all these are but the solace of the wretched and condemned, not the rewards of the blessed." [30]

27 *Idem.*
28 *Idem.*
29 *Ibid.,* pp. 503-4.
30 *Ibid.,* p. 504.

Augustine's emphasis lay on the humane and consolatory significance of Christianity and its doctrine of salvation. Life in this world was a terrifying and miserable experience for man. Happiness could not be found in it. Those who sought anything else than an otherworldly solution for their ills were treading a false path. True, there were aspects of human life in which man's really great intellectual, artistic and moral powers became evident. These provided no true road to happiness, however. Their presence in man was evidence of the continued working of God's creativity even after the Fall. They were imperfect and ultimately unsatisfying. The lure of this world's beauties and pleasures, however, was too powerful and too compelling to the emotions of man to make the Stoic's device of forcing the individual to become indifferent to his feelings an effective one. It was far better to place one's faith in the life eternal and through that faith gain a foretaste of the joy to come in the consoling feeling of hope which true belief brought one even in this life. The importance of Christian otherworldliness, indeed its truth, was proved not by rationally and logically expounding the nature of things but by demonstrating its superior psychological validity in comforting man against the misery, anxiety, fear and mishaps of human life. Aided by divine grace, salvation was achieved emotionally through human willingness to believe. It brought happiness to the individual and was sought by him because of the material and mental insecurity arising from his hazardous relations with his fellow men and the world.

St. Augustine's motivation of the pursuit of happiness in human insecurity has been thus emphasized because it is a major thesis of this study that the humanists, no matter what specific answer they gave to the problem, sought for happiness and discussed the question because their mode of life left them peculiarly insecure in situation and in feeling. In this respect it will be seen that their doctrines were a direct continuation of the Augustinian tradition in medieval thought. Against this discussion of St. Augustine, so closely related in tone to the humanists, the ideas of St. Thomas Aquinas may be set in contrast. Aquinas represented another phase of medieval thought, and it is well to emphasize that it was only one phase. The humanists' revolt against scholasticism may well have been determined by the manner in which the Thomists approached the problem of happiness rather than in any specific disagreement over doctrines. The medieval followers of Augustine were equally bitter enemies of the tradition Thomas defended.

St. Thomas (ca. 1225-1274) expounded his theories of happiness in the first part of the third book of the *Summa Contra Gentiles*.[31] He viewed happiness as a logical and metaphysical rather than a social or psychological problem. He reached the question after a discussion of agents and their ends. Every agent must act for an end and for a good, and since every good is directed toward a higher good, " all things are directed to one end, which is God." [32] All intelligent substances attain to God through their proper operation which is understanding, and therefore, " to know God is the end of every intelligent substance." [33] Since man is an intelligent substance, " the knowledge of God is man's last end. . . . Now the last end of man and of any intelligent substance is called *happiness* or *beatitude* . . . Therefore the last beatitude or happiness of any intelligent substance is to know God." [34] Man can be happy only because of the metaphysically determined circumstance that he happens to be an intelligent substance; as such he must have some last end, which in his case is happiness; since all things have God as a last end, man's happiness or last end must be to attain God according to his proper operation, understanding, that is he must know God.

This is rather sterile and painful language for a human being who finds life difficult and wants to find happiness. St.

---

31 *The Summa Contra Gentiles of St. Thomas Acquinas,* English translation by the English Dominican Fathers, vol. III, London, 1928.

32 *Ibid.,* ch. xvii, pp. 33-36.

33 *Ibid.,* ch. xxv, pp. 56-60.

34 *Ibid.,* p. 60.

Augustine could be much more persuasive to him. Aquinas, however, made no concessions to human feelings. Explicitly he states that happiness has nothing to do with the feelings which come under the will. It is not to be thought that happiness lies in desiring or loving or delighting in God, for " that operation of man whereby he first obtains God is essentially his happiness or beatitude. And this is understanding: since we cannot will what we do not understand. Therefore man's ultimate happiness is essentially to know God by the intellect, and not an act of the will." [35]

It is obvious that to define happiness as the knowledge of God is to deny it to a whole series of other human activities. Aquinas proceeds to explain negatively why happiness must be restricted. First, " it is clearly impossible that human happiness consist in pleasures of the body, the chief of which are pleasures of the table and sex." [36] Such pleasures unite man to things which are by nature below him, and they distract him from contemplation, withdrawing him from intelligible to sensible things.[37] Happiness does not lie in gaining honors because they are conferred by others and may be given to the wicked.[38] It is not in glory because this consists in being known, and it is better actively to know than passively to be known. Glory is an uncertain and unstable thing because it is based on human opinion.[39] Happiness does not lie in wealth because this is sought for the sake of spending it rather than for its own sake. Wealth is a means to liberality and magnanimity which are gained through spending. Wealth is based on chance; it can be lost unwillingly or gained by evil persons.[40] Happiness is not in worldly power because this is based on chance, may be

35 *Ibid.*, ch. xxvi, p. 65.
36 *Ibid.*, ch. xxvi, p. 67.
37 *Ibid.*, pp. 68-69.
38 *Ibid.*, ch. xxviii, pp. 69-70.
39 *Ibid.*, ch. xxix, pp. 70-71.
40 *Ibid.*, ch. xxx, pp. 72-73.

used for evil purposes and rests upon human will and opinion.[41] " Consequently man's happiness consists in no external good; for all external goods, which are known as *goods of chance,* are contained under those we have mentioned." [42]

Neither does happiness lie in goods of the body such as health, beauty and strength, because they pertain to the body which is lower than the soul, may be employed for good or evil, are unstable and are commonly possessed by other animals.[43]

As far as the soul is concerned, it has already been seen that Aquinas denied beatitude could be achieved as a feeling through the will. In addition it was not in the senses because they are lower than the intellect.[44] It is not in acts of moral virtue which are desired not for themselves but for the further end of moderating the passions. It is true that man is man through the possession of reason. Virtue, however, is an effect of reason, and happiness cannot lie in an effect but in reason. Animals too share somewhat in such moral virtues as liberality and fortitude.[45] Thomas' reasons for denying happiness to moral virtues are interesting when compared to those of Augustine and some of the humanists, for they thought the virtues were inadequate because their exercise was disturbing and painful. Happiness is equally lacking in the intellectual virtues of prudence, which is directed toward practical things in the civil life,[46] or of art, which consists in producing things.[47]

" Accordingly if man's ultimate happiness consists not in external things, which are called goods of chance; nor in goods of the body; nor in goods of the soul, as regards the sensitive faculty; nor as regards the intellective faculty, in the practice of moral virtue; nor as regards intellectual virtue in those

41 *Ibid.,* ch. xxxi, pp. 73-74.
42 *Ibid.,* p. 74.
43 *Ibid.,* ch. xxxii, p. 74.
44 *Ibid.,* ch. xxxiii, pp. 74-75.
45 *Ibid.,* ch. xxxiv, pp. 75-76.
46 *Ibid.,* ch. xxxv, pp. 76-77.
47 *Ibid.,* ch. xxxvi, p. 77.

which are concerned about action, namely art and prudence; it remains for us to conclude that man's ultimate happiness consists in the contemplation of the truth." [48]

He does not mean contemplation based on understanding first principles (secular philosophy), for this is merely imperfect potential knowledge, just the beginning of wisdom, and it comes to man by nature and not through study. " Nor does [happiness] consist in contemplation based on the sciences that have the lowest things for their object." Thus the scientist is also excluded.[49] Neither can happiness be gained through the knowledge generally possessed by the majority of men because this knowledge is imperfect and may lead to such erroneous views as that the heavenly bodies are deities or that superior men are gods.[50] It is not in the logician's knowledge acquired by demonstration since that is subject to error.[51] It is equally lacking in the mystic's fervent knowledge of God by faith because this is an act of the will and not of the intellect.[52] As Thomas sought to show by a lengthy refutation of Avicenna and Averroes, knowledge of separate substances is impossible in this life; happiness can therefore not lie in the knowledge of separate substances.[53] Happiness consists in " wisdom, based on consideration of divine things . . . solely in the contemplation of God." [54] Thus he came remarkably close to explicitly proclaiming the activity of the theologian as the sole means to happiness. Actually, of course, his theology compelled him to limit ultimate happiness to the vision of God in the next life. Yet in his denial of happiness to the contemplation of what were to him lower truths a kind of aristocratic intellectualism emerges.

48 *Ibid.*, ch. xxxvii, p. 78.
49 *Ibid.*, p. 79.
50 *Ibid.*, ch. xxxviii, pp. 79-81.
51 *Ibid.*, ch. xxxix, pp. 81-84.
52 *Ibid.*, ch. xl, pp. 84-85.
53 *Ibid.*, chs. xliv-xlv, pp. 100-105.
54 *Ibid.*, p. 79.

Happiness does not seem to be an individual matter for Thomas. Rather it is something achieved by the co-operation of all human activities making possible the vicarious contemplation of truth by the theologian at the pinnacle of a hierarchy. "All other human operations seem to be directed to this as their end. Because perfect contemplation requires that the body should be disencumbered, and to this effect are directed all the products of art that are necessary for life. Moreover it requires freedom from the disturbances of the passions, which is achieved by means of the moral virtues and prudence; and freedom from external disturbance to which all the regulations of the civil life are directed. So that if we consider the matter rightly, we shall see that all human occupations are brought into the service of those who contemplate the truth." [55]

There is lacking in Thomas' theory both the ascetic rigorism of some medieval writers and humanists and the sense of misery and suffering in all lesser activities seen in Augustine's emotional treatment. Here all has its place and graduated degree of importance in the service of the holy community, and though only to a few is the highest function of contemplation open, their work is on behalf of all.

Happiness is achieved in its fullest sense, not in this life,[56] but in the beatific vision of the next, and "in this happy state which results from the divine vision, man's every desire is fulfilled . . ." [57] Then man may know truth and live according to virtue which men pursue in this world "in the occupation of the active and civic life." [58] "Consequent to his life as a citizen, there are also certain goods that man needs for his civic actions. Such is a position of honor . . .", to be well known, to possess riches, to enjoy pleasures.[59] All of these desires, how-

55 *Ibid.*, p. 78.
56 *Ibid.*, ch. xlviii, pp. 111-116.
57 *Ibid.*, p. 148.
58 *Idem.*
59 *Ibid.*, p. 149.

ever, will be fully achieved without involving man in evil only in the next life through contemplation of divine truth.

Although the happiness of those engaged in lower occupations than the contemplation of truth will be achieved for them in the next life, nevertheless, " in this life there is nothing so like this ultimate and perfect happiness as the life of those who contemplate the truth, as far as possible here below . . . For contemplation of truth begins in this life, but will be consummated in the life to come; while the active and civic life does not transcend the limits of this life." [60]

Two features stand out in Thomas' theory of happiness. The first is his characterization of happiness as an act of the intellect which seems to make it an advantage possessed in this world, as far as that is possible, by the theologian exclusively because he more than other men specializes in the use of this faculty for its proper end, the contemplation of the highest truth. The other feature of his theory is that he does not regard the other human faculties nor the other professions of society as directed toward some opposite goal. Thus their exercise need not render the individual miserable or exclude happiness in other professions. This is an important difference between Thomas and Augustine.

The employment of the other faculties and the social division of men into various professions all contributed for Thomas toward making the highest activity of contemplation of truth possible. The other faculties are paths to unhappiness only when they are primarily employed for their own sake and not regarded as means, subordinated one to the other, toward ultimate happiness which all members of Christian society will gain in the next life. The implication is that happiness is not an individual affair but a co-operative social affair. Augustine, however, regarded happiness as essentially individual. In addition he rejected the notion that it was achieved through the intellect but regarded it instead as a matter of feeling. It was gained by an act of the will which, whether acting freely or

60 *Ibid.*, p. 150.

with the aid of grace, brought about the feeling of hope in eternal life in the individual and thus sustained him amid the miseries of the world.

If anything, Thomas came closer to affirming the importance and legitimacy of a wider range of human activities than Augustine and many humanists. The pursuit of both wealth and power were important to sustain the civil life and make acts of charity possible. The only stricture was that these activities were not to be made ends in themselves but directed toward higher goals. When Thomas rejected all but theology as activities conducive to happiness he did not reject them as activities but rather the mistaken notion that by themselves they made for happiness. Augustine, on the other hand, saw in the affects and feelings associated with these activities an inevitable misery for the individual. In this sense Thomas can be considered an optimist about this world and Augustine a pessimist.

Thomas' position was characteristic of the greater integration and security that existed in medieval society or at least in the way the medievals conceived their world. For the individual this would have the result of giving him a sense of the importance of his particular activities or place, since they all fitted into a scheme making for the general salvation of all. However much jealousy may have existed between members of the same social standing or profession, such competitive feelings did not exist theoretically between professions and ranks, since each was recognized for its contribution to the whole. Rivalry, when it existed, would be mitigated by the recognition accorded all places from the most humble to the most high. It is significant that the Franciscans, whose preaching attracted the insecure and disinherited poor, tended to follow Augustine rather than Thomas in theology.

Thomas presents the greater contrast with the humanists because he possessed the feeling of social integration which both they and Augustine lacked. Although the humanists differed widely among themselves, they had one dominant common feature in their individualism. In this respect they departed from the Thomistic consideration of happiness as a social matter and reverted to the earlier phase of Christian thought represented by Augustine, wherein individual salvation and individual happiness played a more central part. In one feature alone they remained true to the main current of scholasticism. Many of them, within quite a different general theory and perspective, reasserted the intellectualism of Thomas. For some, however, the emphasis on the faculty of reason (subordinate to intellect in Thomas' thinking) was made far more exclusive and diametrically opposed to the other faculties which for Thomas were merely subordinate. In this way the humanists were focally concerned with the problem of happiness for the writer, just as in a less emphatic way Thomas indulged in a justification of his own profession of theologian; while the humanists regarded their own profession as something cut off from and in opposition to other professions and thus requiring a special defense, Thomas looked upon theology as dependent upon and the logical outgrowth of all other professions.

CHAPTER III

THE PROBLEM OF LIFE FOR THE HUMANISTS

UNTIL the disastrous events of the early sixteenth century, the Italian humanists showed a strong and persistent interest in the controversies over the end or purpose of man's existence and the conditions under which human destiny had to be worked out. Their attitude toward these questions was characterized principally by their consideration of them from the point of view of the individual trying to understand his place in the world, and abstractly from the point of view of the human species. Although their solutions of these problems differed very little from the solutions offered by medieval writers, in the approach to them from the point of view of the individual or of abstract man, the perspective of the humanists differed widely from the perspective of medieval writers.

In the Middle Ages it was usual for a writer to be associated with some definitely delimited group, association, or organization—a monastic order, a university faculty, an official ecclesiastical position, a gild, a clearly recognized profession such as law or medicine. His membership in an organization, or his position, was publicly and frequently officially recognized and accepted, his place within it stable and comparatively secure. Medieval writers drew in most cases a regular and steady income as a recognized part of their position, or if they practiced a profession, their recompense was in many places regulated by some public body. Therefore, they were usually not confronted concretely with the problem of personal security either in an economic sense or in the sense of wanting some tangible evidence that they were fulfilling a useful and recognized function through their mode of life. Because of these circumstances, when medieval writers approached the problems of the purpose and conditions of human life, they were likely to approach them from the point of view of the association or institution to which they were attached rather than of the individual. The views of Thomas Aquinas are a clear expression of this attitude.

Many of the humanists, on the other hand, had no permanent attachments to any associations or institutions. Excepting those who, like Ambrogio Traversari, were drawn into humanism from a secure ecclesiastical position, the humanists tended to be free-lance writers. Their chief visible means of support was the patronage of some affluent lay or ecclesiastical person. When they were given positions as secretaries or chancellors in a city government or in the court of a lay or ecclesiastical ruler, they pretended that they occupied the position more as a temporary means to the execution of their great literary and philological mission than as the achievement itself of an important social function which they had set out to fulfill. They seemed over-grateful to their patron of the moment for making possible the advance of culture; at the same time they complained of the niggardliness of other great men toward them. The granting of positions to humanists was really a continuation of the haphazard private patronage upon which many of them were dependent.

Perhaps this dependence upon patronage and sinecures forced some of the humanists to face economic insecurity and to become aware that they lacked a genuine and recognized function within society as it was constituted. Many of them in this way may have become peculiarly conscious of the problems of the purpose of human life and the conditions under which it was carried out as they affected the humanists as individuals or as the self-constituted " learned." Another source for this attitude may have been the classical literature read by the humanists. This was mainly of the period after the decline of the Greek City-state and may have infected them with its accentuation of the problem of life for the individual. On the other hand, it is not impossible that their very concern with individual destiny led the humanists to cherish this literature.

Whatever the explanation, these differences between the medieval and the humanist perspective on the problems of life are confirmed by the richness in sociological content of medieval literature and the thinness and rarity of humanist thinking in this direction. The former writers continually wrote specific works or filled their writings with speculations on such subjects as the relations of the three estates to each other, the differences between a healthy and an unhealthy condition of the commonwealth, the comparative importance and difference of functions of the secular and ecclesiastical powers, the future evolution of Christian society up to and beyond the end of the world. The humanists confined themselves to treatises on the abstract merits of tyranny, monarchy and republic, guidebooks on social etiquette and convention, on maintaining a well-ordered household. Humanists such as Machiavelli, who did devote their attention to the problems of the structure and evolution of society, only appeared in the sixteenth century when attention was forced on such problems by the situation of Italy.

It was more common for the humanists to concern themselves with the problems of the individual in making a satisfactory adjustment to society than with the problems of society in general. The problem of individual adjustment, focussing on the single man rather than the group, assumed the general form of seeking the true ends of human existence and of examining the means of realizing these ends. In the humanists' solutions of the problems of individual adjustment the question of how they hoped to find happiness can be answered.

The problem sub-divides into two phases: (1) what is the true nature of man and is this nature well adapted to bringing him happiness? and (2) are the conditions of the world favorable or unfavorable to man as he is constituted? These two phases of the general problem of life will be dealt with separately in the next two chapters. The problem as a whole will be treated first before the specific phases. The humanists viewed the problem as a whole. Moreover, its connection with the manner in which the humanists saw their specific position in society becomes clear in the general treatment. This chapter will consider the attitude of the humanists on life in general, including their explanations of the purposes of life and the possibilities of man's realizing those purposes.

The humanists dealt with these questions in an extraordinarily large number of treatises on such subjects as human happiness, misery, the greatest good. The supreme good was thought to bring happiness to man if it was attained by him, and the end of life was the attainment of the *summum bonum*. They differed in their definitions and conceptions of the supreme good and as to whether it was difficult or easy to gain. Although some of them regarded their own lives favorably and others unfavorably in their definitions, the fact that they were constrained to inquire what the purpose of human life was and how it could be achieved indicates in itself either that they did not feel well enough adjusted and acclimated to the life of their own times to take the answers to these questions for granted or that they felt it highly necessary to justify their own kind of life and their own conclusions about life to their readers.

In the *Secret Conflict of My Desires* [1] Petrarch (1304-1374) showed himself in constant self-conflict, at moments full of resolution to seek worldly fame and full of confidence in the value of his activity, at other moments questioning everything he did or stood for and bitterly condemning himself. The treatise is in the form of a dialogue between his egoistic impulses and his better self personified by St. Augustine. The latter, as Petrarch's conscience, warned over and over again that this life was miserable and that Petrarch should cease trying to find a better condition in it than he possessed.

1 *Secretum de Contemptu Mundi,* English trans. by W. H. Draper, London, 1911. Originally *De secreto conflictu mearum curarum,* but generally denoted by the title given above in the early printed editions.

Giovanni Conversino da Ravenna (1343-1408) wrote about the same time on the *Misery of Human Condition*.[2] The same theme was repeated by the first great humanist Chancellor of the city of Florence, Coluccio Salutati (1331-1406), in a work on *The World and Religion*.[3] At the very end of the fourteenth century the Cardinal, Francesco Zabarella (1366-1417), of humanist leanings, paused long enough in his lectures on canon law to write a treatise on *Happiness*.[4] Happiness was found neither in earthly pleasures, nor in the practice of virtue, but only in the next life by the blessed.[5] Mafeo Vegio (1407-1458) composed a *Dialogue on Happiness and Misery*.[6]

A little later, in the third decade of the fifteenth century, Leonardo Bruni (1369-1444) took up the problem of human happiness in his *Isagogicon of Moral Discipline*.[7] While this views life with more geniality than the preceding works, asserting that it is possible for man to enjoy material and spiritual happiness in this world, happiness is still regarded as difficult to attain. This treatise shows that Bruni also was concerned with the problem of the purpose of human life.

In the case of Lorenzo Valla's (1407-1458) *On Pleasure and the True Good* [8] partial happiness is also seen as possible on

2 *De miseria humanae conditionis*, cited by Baron, *op. cit.*, p. 12 from Cod. IX, 11, fol. 55v-57v of the Querini-Stampaglia library in Venice as a typical work of the later fourteenth century.

3 *De saeculo et religione*, used extensively by Alfred von Martin, *Mittelalterliche Welt-und-Lebensanschauung im Spiegel der Schriften Coluccio Salutatis*, Munich and Berlin, 1913. Von Martin used Cod. Laur. Plut. 53, 4, f. 260 ff. Cf. pp. 33 ff. especially. Also cited by Baron, *op. cit.*, p. 16 in same MS. This work of von Martin's cited hereafter as von Martin II.

4 *De Felicitate Libri Tres*, Padua, 1655. Cf. Gasparo Zonta, *Francesco Zabarella, 1360-1417*, Padua, 1915, pp. 19-21.

5 Zonta, *ibid.*, p. 20. Girolamo Mancini, "Alcune Lettere di Lorenzo Valla," *Giornale storico della letteratura italiana*, XXI (1895), pp. 27-9.

6 *De felicitate et miseria dialogus*, in *Dialogi decem variorum auctorum*, s.l., 1473, fol. 66 ff.

7 *Isagogicon moralis disciplinae*, pp. 20-41, Hans Baron, *Leonardo Bruni Aretinos Humanistische-Philosophische Schriften*, Leipzig, 1928.

8 *De Voluptate ac de Vero Bono Libri Tres*, Basel, 1519; also in *Opera*

earth. This work takes three of the current views on happiness and contrasts them. Written in 1432, it was Valla's reply to Zabarella, Vegio, Bruni and the vulgarization of Epicureanism typified in the attitude of such a writer as Antonio Panormità.[9]

Twenty years later Poggio Bracciolini (1380-1459) composed one of the dourest works of the entire century—*The Misery of Human Condition*.[10] At the ripe old age of seventy-two, after a successful life, when a certain mellowness would seem natural, Poggio let forth this sustained complaint against everything that this world might offer a man.

About the same time Poggio's friend, Bartolommèo Fazio (1400?-1457), wrote on *The Happiness of Man*.[11] For him too, few earthly careers had much to offer; only in religion and spiritual goods might man find a degree of solace.

Later in the century Marsilio Ficino (1433-1499) had an argument over *Happiness* with Lorenzo de' Medici (1449-1492) and recorded his views in a letter on the subject.[12] Lorenzo also put down his views in a poem.[13] Ficino rejected all sides of worldly existence and found happiness only in the mystical pleasure of the soul in the beatific vision. Another member of the Florentine Neoplatonic circle, Cristoforo Landino (1424-1504), took up the same problem of the purpose of human life in his *Camaldulensian Disputations*.[14]

Omnia, Basel (Henricpetri) 1540, which is followed by Max von Wolff, *Lorenzo Valla Sein Leben und Seine Werke*, Leipzig, 1893, pp. 13-36.

9 *Cf*. Girolamo Mancini, *Vita di Lorenzo Valla*, Florence, 1891, Chap. 2.

10 *De Miseria Humanae Conditionis Libri II, Opera Omnia*, Basel, 1538, pp. 86-131.

11 *De viri felicitate, seu summi boni fruitione*, Leyden, 1628; also in *Dialogi decem variorum auctorum*, s.l. 1473 and separately, Antwerp, 1556. Discussed by Lynn Thorndike, *Science and Thought in the Fifteenth Century*, New York, 1929, pp. 185-187.

12 *Epistola de felicitate, Opera Omnia*, Basel, 1576 (second edition by Henricpetri but pagination same as in first), I, pp. 662-65.

13 According to Paulus Oscarius Kristeller, *Supplementum Ficinianum*, Florence, 1937, vol. I, p. xciv. This was probably *Lauda*, I, "O Dio, o sommo bene, or come fai?" in *Opere*, Florence, 1825, vol. III, pp. 79-82.

14 *Disputationum Camaldulensium libri quattuor*, Venice, 1500; Book I, "De vita activa et contemplativa", and Book II, "De summo bono."

Platina (Bartolommeo de Sacchi) (1421-1481) described his emotional struggle to become reconciled to the hard path of this life in his *Dialogues on True and False Good*.[15] These dialogues debate the questions of happiness and the true end of man.

Shortly after he was driven out of Florence, Francesco Filelfo (1398-1481) mourned the fate of himself and of others of similar misfortune in a tract on *Exile*.[16] Near the end of his life he took up the question of the true end of man in *Five Books on Moral Discipline*.[17]

Also appearing in the second half of the fifteenth century were three works, known only in manuscript, which have been described by Lynn Thorndike.[18] Giovanni Nesi (fl. 1485) concluded in his treatise on *Morals*[19] that man could gain some happiness in the possession of the goods of the world. Gregory Crispus (fl. 1475) claimed that *The Cultivation of Humanism and Virtue*[20] was a means toward the achievement of the supreme good which was the love of God. Oliver of Sienna (fl. 1490) considered the problem of the purpose of life among many other subjects in a brief treatise, which Thorndike has compared to medieval *compendia*, on *God and the Principles of Natural Things and Supreme Bliss*.[21]

15 *De falso et vero bono dialogi tres,* in *De Vitis ac Gestis Summorum Pontificum . . . Eiusdem item Platinae,* etc., Cologne, 1551, pp. 1-30 (*De Vitis* etc. comes first and is numbered separately; several opuscula, of which the above is the first, follow and are numbered consecutively).

16 *Commentationes Florentinae de Exilio,* Cod. Magliab. VI, 209 (II, 70). *Cf.* Carlo Errera, " Il ' Commentationes Florentinae de Exilio ' di Francesco Filelfo," *Archivio Storico Italiana,* Series 5, Tomo 5, 1890, pp. 193-227.

17 *De morali disciplina libri quinque,* Venice, 1552.

18 Thorndike, *op. cit.,* chap. XI, " Some Renaissance Moralists and Philosophers." He also discussed along with these works Bartolommeo Fazio, *De viri felicitate* which, however, has been printed more than once. See below, pp. 94-96.

19 *De moribus,* Cod. Laur. Plut. 77, 24. Thorndike, pp. 187-91.

20 *De cultu humanitatis et honestatis libellus,* Cod. Laur. Plut., 77, 17. Thorndike, pp. 181-5.

21 *De deo et rerum naturalium principiis et summa beatitudine,* Cod. Laur. Plut. 82, 21. Thorndike, pp. 191-3.

The age old problem of the perversity of justice in this world where the evil were rewarded and the good persecuted was debated and the way of the world at length justified by Matteo Bosso (1427-1502) on *Adversities to be Borne*.[22] Late in the fifteenth century Filippo Beroaldo (1453-1505) considered the possibilities of man being happy in an *Oration on Happiness* and concluded that the conditions of the world did not permit its achievement.[23] Two decades later Pietro Alcyonio (1487?-1527) in a work on *Exile*[24] discussed the ways in which a learned man might reduce its sorrows and discomforts. After the Sack of Rome, Piero Valeriano (1477-1550) wrote his famous work on the plight of the humanists, *The Unhappiness of Men of Letters*.[25]

These treatises do not show complete discouragement about the chances of achieving happiness in this world. But even those which admit, either that worldly success is no obstacle to contentment, or that there is a favorable possibility of gaining worldly success, are not unequivocally affirmative or this-worldly in their argument. For Leonardo Bruni, virtue was as important an ingredient of happiness as good health and sufficient means; in fact the last was important rather as a means to the first than for its own sake. The capacity for virtue, furthermore, was not a natural power, shared equally by everyone, but something with which some individuals were better endowed than others, so that even the desire and means for virtue were no guarantee of happiness.[26] Lorenzo Valla was also not completely a voluptuary.[27] Almost all of the other writers were in some degree disturbed by the difficulty of find-

22 *De Tolerandis Adversis Dialogus,* Florence, 1492?

23 *De Felicitate Opusculum,* Bologna, 1495 and fol. cxii-cxxii, *Opuscula Varia Philippi Beroaldi,* Basel, 1513.

24 *Medices Legatus, sive de Exsilio Libri Duo,* Venice, 1522 and in J. B. Menckenius, *Analecta de Calamitate,* Leipzig, 1707.

25 *De Litteratorum Infelicitate Libri Duo,* Geneva, 1821, also in Menckenius, *op. cit.*

26 See below, pp. 111-112.

27 See below, pp. 115-116.

ing individual security, or pressed to find some justification for the difficulty. An undercurrent of dissatisfaction and perplexity over the adjustments that the individual had to make with this life runs through the writings of the humanists. It was, perhaps, inevitable that definite expressions of antagonism to worldly values should at times rise to the surface.

One of the forms which the humanists' concern over their career and life in this world assumed was a debate over the nature of true nobility. This term, which had originally a primarily social content, very early acquired its ethical and psychological meaning as well. In an environment, which took human inequality for granted, the mode of life of a person who occupied a superior social position or was preeminent in some other way came to be thought of as the norm of the proper way to conduct one's life. If an individual was driven to doubt the propriety or importance of his own kind of life, or if he found that ready recognition of the worth of his mode of existence was not prevalent, he could set his own mind at ease or convince his neighbors by showing that nobility in its " real " or " true " sense coincided with his own life. Thus a discussion of nobility is likely to grow out of a feeling of insecurity.

The adjective *noble* nowadays more usually connotes ethical respectability than lofty birth. This spiritualized meaning has gradually grown out of the debates that arose from the circumstances just described. These debates occurred among the Troubadours in the twelfth and thirteenth centuries when, in order to place the poets on the same social level as the great ladies of the courts, with whom they were associating, nobility was defined as the possession of virtue. The theme was carried over into Italy and taken up in a similar way by Dante.[28] It was later applied to their own circumstances by the humanists, and the debate was still being carried on by the *Honnêtes*

28 Karl Vossler, *Die Philosophischen Grundlagen zum " sussen neuen stil "*, Heidelberg, 1904, pp. 24-41, " Die Adelfrage."

Hommes of the French salons of the seventeenth century.[29] In the following treatises the theme reflects the uncertainty of the humanists both about the adequacy of the conditions under which they existed and about the importance in the eyes of mankind of the activities in which they engaged.

The life of the man of the world who had wealth and a good name was contrasted with the life of the man of virtue and learning who has no wealth and an obscure background by Buonaccorso da Montemagno, Jr. (1391?-1429) in a very popular treatise on *Nobility*.[30] In the form of a debate before the Roman Senate between two suitors for the hand of a lady, one of whom satisfies the first and the other the second definition of nobility, the outcome is left undecided, although it is clear where the author's sympathies lay. The argument that nobility was inherited was based primarily on the idea that the children of great men inherit not only the physical beauty, strength and appearance, but also the moral and intellectual qualities of their ancestors. The children should be honored with nobility as a means of paying off the debt owed to the ancestors for their services to the community. It was also the opinion of the vulgar that nobility was inherited.[31]

Wealth also confers nobility because it makes possible liberality and the practice of virtues which the impoverished person is in no position to exercise. Through wealth one's virtue becomes known; in poverty it remains obscure. The wealthy man

29 Maurice Magendie, *La politesse mondaine et les théories des honnêtetés, en France au XVIIe siecle, de 1600-1660*, Paris, 1925, Part II, chaps. 9-11, pp. 339-85; Part V, chap. 11, pp. 823-8; Part VI, chap. 7.

30 The edition used attributes the work to Leonardo Bruni: *Leonardi Aretini opusculum . . . de nobilitate*, s.l.a., but the British Museum Catalogue lists it as Milan, 1480. The leaves are unnumbered but the copy in the British Museum is numbered in pencil fol. 1-24. Hans Baron, *Leonardo Bruni* etc., *op. cit.*, pp. 180 ff. on a comparison of *MSS* decides that it is the work of Buonaccorso to whom about half of the editions attribute it. The ideas expressed in it are also quite foreign to Bruni. Baron gives a long list of MSS and printed editions.

31 *Op. cit.*, fol. 3b-6a.

of high birth could offer villas in the suburbs, luxuries, many servants, a wide circle of friends, beautiful surroundings.[32]

Against this argument it is urged that it takes no account of the merits of the person in question. Many persons of low birth have become great men, e.g. Cicero, Cato, Socrates, Euripides and the early Scipios. On the other hand, the descendants of great families have often been wicked, disgraceful, or obscure. Virtue and nobility come only by one's own labor, since the soul, the seat of virtue, is not inherited and is superior to the body. Many great and noble men lived in poverty as well. Poverty and nobility can exist side by side. Liberality and all virtues can be practiced without the aid of wealth. The person who devotes himself to the study of letters and philosophy, who seeks the company of scholars, who desires and fears nothing, who lives in humble circumstances is truly noble.[33] " What is more blissful in human affairs than to carry on life in the most tranquil enjoyment of virtue and good morals? What sweeter than to be able to nourish genuine talent in the best and most beautiful meditations? . . . Today, indeed, character contends with immodesty, continence with lust, magnanimity with indolence, learning with ignorance, virtue with sloth." [34] Which of these two modes of life is the nobler?

In this discussion of nobility, as in the following ones, the problem of the social position of the humanists is very closely involved with the problem of making a satisfactory adjustment to the life of the period. Clearly Buonaccorso was trying here to say that the activities of the humanist were just as much entitled to respect and recognition as the way of life of the prominent man of wealth and family for whom the humanist

32 *Ibid.*, fol. 6b-9b.

33 *Ibid.*, fol. 9b-24a.

34 *Ibid.*, fol. 24b, " Quid ne beatius in rebus humanis est quam in tranquilissima virtutis iocunditate ac moribus vitam agere? Quid dultius quam posse in optimis ac pulcherrimis cogitationibus verax ingenium alere? . . . Hodie quidem honestas cum impuditicia, continentia cum libidine, magnanimitas cum secordia, eruditia cum inscientia, virtus cum ignavia contendit."

carried on his work. The fact that he rationalized the humanist way of life as that of the truly noble person indicates, perhaps, that he felt it necessary to do so because the humanist was denied the respectability and the comforts which the other variety of nobleman had as a matter of course. Lacking wealth or social standing, insecure because of that lack, he repudiated what he desired and embraced the poverty which he feared.

The argument over nobility was almost the same argument as that carried on over happiness. Nobility and happiness were defined by many humanists in the same way and tended to be identified. The result was a denial of the validity of the goods of this world and was in this sense pessimistic. The humanists who accepted this definition of nobility were greatly influenced by Stoicism in their attitudes on happiness, and this definition made use of the Stoic device of " willing what exists " instead of employing the this-worldly strategy of " shaping outside circumstances according to their desires." [35]

The discussion of *True Nobility* by Platina, although chronologically later than the work of Poggio discussed below, follows the arguments of Buonaccorso very closely and should logically come next.[36] The connection between thought about nobility and happiness is very clearly indicated in this work, for it starts with the usual problem discussed in the treatises on happiness: the nature of the supreme good.[37] Platina was amazed at the error of thinking that the supreme good lies in riches, power and honors. It never comes " from lust for fortune and the free will of man." The Crassus of today is frequently the Codrus of tomorrow. The ill fortune of famous Romans should give one pause. " The supreme good is that which always maintains itself in the same way and which cannot be impelled hither and yon by the winds of fortune." It consists of virtue alone and cannot be acquired without

35 Bevan, *op. cit.*, p. 29.

36 *De vera nobilitate* in *De Vitis ac Gestis* etc. *op. cit.*, pp. 52-64.

37 See below, pp. 90-92 for Platina's discussion of happiness.

wisdom.[38] The question of true nobility finally arose out of a discussion of affluent and noble persons who are depraved. Like the supreme good, true nobility is acquired from nothing other than virtue.[39]

As in Buonaccorso's work the arguments in favor of nobility of birth and wealth come first. Nobility must be inherited, just as superior livestock comes from well-bred animals. The honors customarily paid to ancestors and the respect of children for their parents are indications that nobility is inherited. Both the desire for glory, and wealth, honors and servants are inherited. Inherited wealth makes beneficence possible. As Aristotle had reasoned, liberality and virtue are impossible without facilities wherewith to practice them. Nobility consists of having an old family together with inherited and acquired wealth.[40]

This argument was held to be incorrect, " for nobility, as it pleases the Stoics, is a certain splendor arising from nothing else than virtue itself by means of which we may distinguish the good from the evil and the worthy from the unworthy." [41] The noble person is he who can conquer cupidity and coerce avarice, " even if he should be born from the lowest lot of men." [42] Rulers and subjects are born in exactly the same way and differ from each other only in their virtue and vice. There are many examples of great men of low birth and of evil men of high birth. The degeneracy of the descendants of great families and the condemnation of the faults and crimes of their

38 *Op. cit.,* p. 52, ". . . ex libidine fortunae ac hominum arbitrio . . . illud esse summum bonum quod semper eodem modo sese habet, quodque fortunae procellis impelli hac et illuc non potest."

39 *Ibid.,* pp. 54-5 (misprinted 42, 45).

40 *Ibid.,* pp. 55-6 (misprinted 45, 44).

41 *Ibid.,* p. 57, " Nobilitas enim, ut Stoicis placet, est splendor quidam non aliunde veniens, quam ex ipsa virtute, qua bonum a malo, dignum ab indigno secludamus."

42 *Ibid.,* p. 58, ". . . etiamsi ex infima sorte hominum natus fuerit."

children by illustrious parents show conclusively that nobility has nothing to do with high birth.[43]

Nobility is also joined with poverty. By poverty, not destitution or beggary, but contentment with very little is meant. This is true wealth. Man is not born rich; food and drink are sufficient for him. The Romans were praised for their poverty; calamities followed the growth of avarice among them. Liberality and beneficence are possible for the poor man, since public services and other gifts are greater than money. Wealth and honor are constantly changing hands, whereas virtue is constant. The tyrant frequently appears liberal by plundering the many to reward a few satellites and favorites. The truly noble person scorns the goods of fortune, overcomes all desires, and is versed in charity, justice, fortitude, dignity, candor, gravity, prudence and wisdom.[44]

In both of these treatises on nobility the position of the Stoics, which confined value to the exercise of the reason, was taken. In spite of the lack of material comforts and social recognition a truly virtuous person might find security in this life. But it was in reality a retreat from the world, since it was offered as a consolation for the difficulty of gaining and keeping those very things that the majority of mankind desired and recognized as worthy. Platina insisted that one must rationalize one's miseries " lest we follow the ignorant crowd which very frequently falls into the greatest of errors and whose opinion rarely agrees with wisdom." [45]

The Stoic position also tacitly admitted that it would have been comforting to have the goods of this world, for it emphasized the difficulty of retaining them, and at the same time preferred to use poverty as a figure of speech for a life of modest means rather than of literal destitution. Clearly the Stoicism of some of the humanists, here broached in their

43 *Ibid.*, pp. 58-9.

44 *Ibid.*, pp. 60-4.

45 *Ibid.*, p. 60, ". . . ne ignarum vulgus sequamur, qui persaepe in maximos errores dilabitur, cuiusque opinio raro cum sapientia convenit."

treatises on nobility as an answer to their quest for social recognition, indicates how far they were from the egotist's attitude that anyone, if he had the will and perseverance, could
gain a position of security and esteem for himself in worldly
society.

Poggio Bracciolini's treatise on *Nobility* [46] contains all of
the arguments used by Buonaccorso and Platina with much
more elaboration and concreteness of detail. In the form of a
dialogue, Lorenzo de' Medici (the brother of Cosimo) upholds
the view that nobility comes from family and wealth combined
with virtue, and Nicolò Niccoli the view that it consists of
virtue alone. Lorenzo rests his argument on " what the crowd
holds, which has the greatest authority in matters of this
sort." [47]

Niccoli opposes right reason to opinion, which varies with
time and place. Even in Italy there is the greatest difference between the accepted notions of nobility in Naples, Venice, Rome,
Florence and Genoa. In Naples only the descendants of the
original houses who engage neither in trade nor agriculture are
considered noble. In Venice the nobility is a faction of the
people composed of those who engage in trade and belong to
the Senate. The Roman nobility despise trade but admit wealth
acquired in rural occupations. In Florence the descendants of
old families who hold public office are noble. The Genoese
have the same custom as the Venetians. The Lombards, Germans, French, English, Spanish and Greeks have still different
opinions. If customs differ so much, they can not have the same
origin. Since trade comes in for so much vituperation by wise
men, it certainly cannot confer nobility; nor is the artisan
noble. Wealth, whether acquired or inherited, is not necessarily
accompanied by virtue, so it cannot confer nobility. The worst
sort of men seek public offices, honors and dignities. Old families produce wicked men. Besides, descent should make every-

---

46 *De nobilitate* in *Opera Omnia,* Basel, 1538, pp. 64-83.

47 *Ibid.,* p. 66, ". . . quod vulgus tenet, qui in eiusmodi rebus plurimum
auctoritatis possidet."

one equally noble, since all have ancestors going back a thousand years. Agriculture is more healthy and neutral in regard to nobility, but it frequently consumes one's entire energy. Nobility does not come from a military life or knighthood, which only bring the vain pomp of uniforms and decorations. It is not in the solitary and stupid leisure of the northern nobility, which is frequently combined with banditry and confers no chance of practicing virtue.[48]

Nobility can only be defined rationally and logically. Things are either good, evil or indifferent. Nobility is obviously not evil. If it were in goods, it could be in goods of fortune, of the body or of the soul. The possessors of the goods of fortune are not noble but wealthy. It is not in the goods of the body, for then an unhealthy or an ugly person cannot be noble. The goods of the soul are virtues, but single virtues do not confer nobility. Prudence makes a man prudent, wisdom wise, and so on. Nobility is not in indifferent things, because it would then be both good and evil. It is either in man or in things. If in man by nature, everyone is noble; if by acquisition, it comes from actions, and actions make one good, evil, prudent or wealthy, but not noble. If it were in things, nobility would come and go, be gained and lost like riches. Therefore it seems to be nothing except a form of ostentation.[49]

Poggio did not end his treatise on this surprisingly cynical and nihilistic note. He would have been completely subversive of life if he had, for then he would have admitted that there was no possible goal toward which men could legitimately strive in this world. His position would have been close to that of the ancient Cynics.

Lorenzo then accuses Niccoli of opposing not only vulgar opinion but the opinion of the wise. This leads Niccoli to shift his position and return to his former argument that nobility lies in virtue alone in accord with the Stoics and in opposition both to Aristotle and to the Cynics. Against Aristotle's defini-

48 *Ibid.*, pp. 66-72.
49 *Ibid.*, pp. 72-3.

tion of nobility as the combination of old riches and virtues, Niccoli argues that virtuous poor men are frequently great, that riches are under the *arbitrium* of fortune and can be given and taken away whereas nobility has to be constant, that riches are gained by evil means whereas nobility requires virtue, that virtue comes of one's own actions and cannot be inherited since the children of the wicked may turn out virtuous. Thus nobility according to Aristotle's definition either cannot exist or cannot be inherited. Even if his definition were accepted, the combination of wealth and virtue is extremely rare and easily lost. Against Lorenzo's argument that virtue cannot be practiced without wealth and that poverty leads to the corruption of virtue, Niccoli urges that only depraved men place poverty among the worst evils and that actually it is the pursuit of riches which renders men vicious and criminal. Even Aristotle admitted the rarity of virtue in a wealthy man.[50]

Niccoli does not follow Diogenes, the Cynic, who catered to the crowd and condemned all nobility, but the Stoics, who followed the precepts of reason and found nobility in virtue alone. They derived their ideas from Plato, who said the best variety of nobility was that of the men who had gained it by their own virtue and greatness of soul. The Stoics added to this that only the wise man can be noble.[51]

Lorenzo replies with an attack on the Stoic conception of morality. Many have praised it, but few have desired it. Wealth, family and public activity are necessary unless the civil life is to be avoided. The philosopher, content with his studies in a tiny library, or the sober, pious, chaste, wise man, living away from the world in some *villula* might be virtuous but certainly not noble.[52] But from Niccoli's Stoic point of view the advantages of the city, of wealth, family and public office are indifferent with respect to nobility. The philosopher, though he lives meagerly and alone, if he adds to human well-

50 *Ibid.*, pp. 74-8.
51 *Ibid.*, pp. 70-80.
52 *Ibid.*, pp. 81-82.

being and good by his studies and vigils, is the truly noble person.[53]

All three treatises on nobility tend to identify nobility with the life of the humanists as they conceived themselves. All idealize the manner in which they were forced to be different from the rest of society and emphasize the rarity of this virtuous and poor type of wise man. Although this company of sages lacked the apparatus of a worldly life of distinction, they regarded themselves as being far superior to the rest of mankind because they were distinguished in being guided by reason rather than opinion and emotion. The first impulse is to say, on these grounds, that they achieved as they claimed, far greater security than those who had an ample supply of material comforts and the recognition of the crowd. This snobbish attitude would be definitely a sign of confidence on the part of the humanists and of an ability to rise above and resolve the difficulties of life.

Another interpretation, however, is possible. Perhaps the popularity of the Stoic attitude among the humanists was more truly a counsel of desperation. If this point of view really brought them security, why should they be so anxious to point out how they differed from other men, how they were better, how the vulgar were deceiving themselves in their ignorance? There is little compassion, pity or sympathy for humanity in general. Rather there is hostility, sneering and blame. The Stoic attitude might well have been a defense arising out of a sense of the shortcomings of their life either as far as physical comforts or as far as having a genuine and constructive place in society were concerned. In accord with such an interpretation their attitude might have had a double motive: to rationalize and convince themselves that their life was as it ought to be and to demonstrate to others that they were worthy of recognition and support. It may be doubted whether the humanists would have turned down a gift from a patron or refused to trade on their family name, if they had a reputable

53 *Ibid.*, pp. 82-3.

one. The humanists' definition of nobility to fit their own situation may very well have been symptomatic of a feeling of hesitation and doubt about the conditions of life. At least there can be no doubt that they were keenly aware of the difficulties in the way of achieving and maintaining a secure place in the world. Their requirements for a secure place were constancy and tranquillity, and freedom from the assaults of the environment, rather than the power and creative shaping of the environment to meet their individual purposes (which they perhaps secretly desired and concealed behind the ideal). At the same time their identification of their own ideal of life with nobility reveals the aristocratic character of their attitude.

Alfred von Martin has carefully worked out the reasonings involved in this humanist ideal of life as they are found in the writings of Coluccio Salutati,[54] and this analysis helps to clarify the combination of pessimism and snobbish aloofness found in the treatises on nobility. For this reason it is useful to repeat part of it. Von Martin's treatment of humanist Stoicism is more convincing than Baron's. The latter's classification of Salutati as one of the poor fourteenth century humanists [55] who idealized their own poverty breaks down when it is considered that Salutati was a very successful person by worldly standards and occupied the Florentine Chancellory for a long time. The conflict between his actual career and his ideal life was very apparent. He is thus a good person to study in the hope of arriving at a better understanding of some of the later humanists.

Salutati's ideal, according to von Martin, was to achieve virtue by means of moral philosophy and humanistic studies instead of logic and metaphysics. Thus the ideal of the Christian Middle Ages was retained while the means were rejected.[56] From the ancient writers those were chosen who came closest

54 Von Martin, I, *op. cit.*

55 Baron, *op. cit.,* p. 16.

56 Von Martin, I, pp. 76-7. Salutati, however, saw the value of disputation in the field of morals.

to the otherworldly ethics of the Middle Ages, namely the Stoics, Cicero and especially Seneca. " Here as there the turning of the sense away from the world seemed to be preached before all else; and the disposition toward a ' new flight from the world ' especially came to meet this ideal."[57] Much more than Petrarch, Salutati considered the monastic state the ideal one. For a time he identified the Stoic morality with the Christian. External goods were transitory goods for both Stoic and Christian, so he found the former's supreme good to be the latter's eternal good.[58] He considered Petrarch the ideal representative of both ideals because " ' he hated wealth and power and full of humility renounced external honors.' " [59] To both philosophy and religion death was no evil; Stoic apathy and Christian humility were the same; fate and providence were identified.[60] Later Salutati came to feel that Stoicism was lacking in human feeling and too rigorous and cold, especially in its attitude toward death. Death was a great torture and, as such, either a punishment or a trial. Thus he came to renounce Stoicism and embrace in theory the Christian position that salvation could be gained only through the grace of God and was beyond all human powers.[61]

Out of this experience grew Salutati's intellectualized conception of virtue, that was to be so common among humanists. Virtue was conceived of as being the means to eternal felicity in the next life, and in this sense was otherworldly. It also came to be considered as a means to happiness in this world. Virtue, however, was defined as the pursuit of knowledge and beauty of form. Thus the ideal life was the humanist one, dedicated to studies.[62] Through an assimilation of the Christian morality with the world-despising ideal of the Stoics, the new humanist

57 *Ibid.*, p. 77.
58 *Ibid.*, pp. 78-9.
59 *Ibid.*, pp. 79-80.
60 *Ibid.*, pp. 80-2.
61 *Ibid.*, pp. 82-92.
62 *Ibid.*, pp. 92-4.

ideal of virtue came forth. But like the monastic ideal, it was pessimistic and implied rejection of the world, for " concern with knowledge in and for itself is ' virtue ' because it draws the sense away from the valueless, material, transitory goods toward the alone valuable, enduring, spiritual goods." [63] To the Stoic, virtue alone is good; to the Christian, thought on our immortality; to the humanist, study meant both virtue and care for the eternal, and thus this ideal united the Stoic and Christian ideals. Erudition alone was a worthy object for human endeavor; everything else was either indifferent or harmful.[64] Therefore, physical love must be avoided and only spiritualized love allowed. Power, honors, riches must be shunned.[65] Since study was virtue, it contributed to one's own good and to the good of others. As a means to the latter, eloquence had to be cultivated. But as knowledge, from being a means to virtue, came to be identified with virtue, so eloquence, from being the means to spreading virtue, came to be considered virtue itself.[66]

This ideal of Salutati's, like that of the other humanists (as shown in their works on *Nobility,* discussed above, and on the *Dignity of Man,* discussed below), involved a turning away from worldly values and so reflected a negative feeling about this life. Similarly, Salutati's ideal also involved an aristocratic attitude, the feeling that this way of life was superior to that of other men. Knowledge and eloquence were the " proper gifts of man by which he is distinguished from other animate creatures." [67] The educated man is in " higher degree human than the uneducated." The wise and eloquent men " stand higher above other men than man through the possession of reason stands above the animal." The new ideal is the medieval ideal of the world-flight made this-worldly. " One flees the

63 *Ibid.,* p. 95.
64 *Ibid.,* p. 96.
65 *Ibid.,* pp. 96-101.
66 *Ibid.,* pp. 102-05.
67 *Ibid.,* p. 106.

' masses,' the great crowd of uneducated people from whom
virtue along with culture is absent." " Thus a new segregated
class was formed which, like the monastic class, felt itself as
an elite, elevated far above the mass of other men."[68] Virtue
and learning were the only criteria of a man's worth. The only
division between men was that between the educated and the
uneducated. Office, high birth, or wealth meant nothing; the
uneducated noble of the older types belonged to the vulgar
mass.[69] The true sign of nobility, for Salutati, like the writers
analyzed above, was the obligation of virtue, which meant devotion to studies. The old nobility were valued only according
to their devotion to studies.[70]

As the humanists drew away from other men, they drew
closer to each other. The humanists had a community of interest
against the vulgar. So they developed a solidarity among themselves. A cult of friendship of those especially devoted to virtue
and study grew up. It was an obligation of virtue to maintain
friendship with the other men of virtue, and this was a means
to the highest earthly satisfaction. Salutati also considered it a
religious duty, for humanist friendship corresponded to the
Christian love of one's neighbor. By praising each other the rewards of virtue might be obtained through the fame that would
thus come to one. Salutati felt at times that fame was an unworthy thing and an un-Christian end, but tended to favor it.[71]
His letters to supposedly close friends showed him to be chiefly
interested in praising or criticizing his own or their practice of
virtue (i.e. style) even where it concerned a highly personal
and emotional matter.[72] There was nothing personal about this
cult of friendship; instead it was conceived as a means of

68 *Ibid.*, p. 107. Von Martin ignores the similar feeling of superiority
of the university men of the Middle Ages. His analysis of Salutati seems
accurate, but it is not right to call Salutati's ideas new except in their sharpness and greater elaboration. *Cf.* Thomas' praise of the theologian above,
pp. 34-36.
69 *Ibid.*, pp. 108-09.
70 *Ibid.*, p. 110.
71 *Ibid.*, pp. 111, 121.
72 *Ibid.*, p. 194.

carrying out the ideal of virtue.[73] It provided a means of demonstrating one's virtuous knowledge of moral philosophy and virtuous style through the circulation of letters. The latter device "served far less to maintain 'friendly' relationships than the maintenance of the relationships served the writing of letters: one needed those relationships in order to be able to peddle out one's knowledge before a grateful and steadily and cheerfully applauding public and at the same time to parade with eloquence."[74]

Von Martin thought that this ideal of Salutati's found little corroboration in his actual life, for he was actually very much concerned with securing a solid, material reward for his endeavors. Salutati revealed his motives for the exaggerated conception of the position of the humanist and the importance of his activities. Insecurity and lack of a general recognition explained his aristocratic notions. It was a bad age which failed to recognize the value of studies: " all had sense only for material values, for money and money profit, therefore the 'good' [i.e. the humanists] had doubly firmly to hang together."[75] Both the belief that, because he was indifferent to worldly values and anxious only about his virtue and study, he occupied a superior position as the truly noble person, and the cult of humanist friendship, were needed by the humanist to help him achieve a sense of solidarity and some sort of a feeling of confidence in the face of material and psychological insecurity. The ideal was too unrealistic to be actually followed in life. It was not a sign of bold trust in one's own ability to get on in this world nor a sign of genuine belief in the actual importance of one's activities, but rather a psychological defense against demoralization.

Probably this idealization of the humanists' lack of security contributed to building up self-respect. Von Martin showed how Salutati repressed all warm feelings of sympathy toward

73 *Ibid.*, pp. 182-206.
74 *Ibid.*, p. 206.
75 *Ibid.*, p. 196.

his family and his friends.[76] " This man seemed incapable of giving himself over to an unrestrained feeling." In this way, at least, he was able to approach his ideal in actual life, for " Salutati's disposition of character, his tendency toward the reasonable, his lack of deep feeling and tender sensibility coincided here with the Christian-ascetic point of view . . ." [77] He was thus enabled to keep up appearances and gain respect for himself, since " he conducted himself not as a blinded pagan but as the best of the Romans in such a model way that he needed no admonition. The people should know that !" [78]

Another advantage of his ideal was that it gave the humanist an argument that might induce possible patrons to grant him position and treat him with respect. Von Martin showed how eagerly Salutati courted the ruling powers in the hope of support. " Thus he now felt it as especially grievous that even the socially ruling classes, nobles and princes, opposed all intellectual activities so equally that they indeed had liking for luxury, hunting, falconry, jousting and war but not for the ' study of letters ', indeed that they even ' held it to be below their class (servile) to be concerned with the free arts which once, because it was found that they only suited the free born, were rightly named the " free " ' . . . In a melancholy mood Salutati seemed to fear even the decline of the studies, just awakened to a new life, from the lack of a patronage system." [79] It was this fear of going unsupported and unrecognized, this craving to find regular, stable means of support and position in society such as the medieval writer who was attached to an institution enjoyed, that seems to have been the ruling motive for the curious combination of the ideal of withdrawing from the world to make the most of one's lack with the haughty elevation of this kind of life above that of other men. If security were to be gained, it had to be gained from the ruling powers,

76 *Ibid.*, pp. 171-186.
77 *Ibid.*, p. 173.
78 *Ibid.*, p. 175.
79 *Ibid.*, p. 207.

and they might take notice if humanism were made to appear noble itself. Meanwhile, some comfort might be gotten from the sense of self-righteousness this attitude gave one.

Aristocratic, pessimistic Neostoicism was the product of the merging of a compulsion to turn one's back upon and withdraw from the difficulties of life, repressing all normal feelings, and of a compulsion to make the most of these difficulties and utilize the very detachment, insecurity and lack of recognition of the humanist to gain fixed, secure, recognized position. This was Salutati's strategy at a time when humanism had not yet achieved position and recognition. It was the strategy of some of his successors. That this attitude found successors would seem to indicate both that it was a means toward success and that the need for it, even later when conditions were more favorable, continued to exist. The fact that there were also writers who viewed things more sanguinely a little later might mean that the need was not quite so pressing in the middle of the fifteenth century as it had been earlier. Apart from the details of the development of this tendency, one impression stands out. From the very beginning through the high point of humanism, personal security was a crucial problem for the Italian humanists regardless of how it was solved. The solutions tended, further, to limit human action in many cases, although broader attitudes were by no means lacking.

The concern of the humanists over the purpose and conditions of human life, which was illustrated in the attitudes of Salutati and of the authors of treatises on *Nobility*, found a different form of expression with a correspondingly different attitude in works on the *Dignity and Excellence of Man*.[80] The treatises written on this subject are closer to the traditional Christian glorification of man as the principal result of the

---

80 Bartolommeo Fazio, *De excellentia et praestantia hominis,* in Felino Sandeo, *De Regibus Siciliae et Apuliae epitome ad Alex. VI*, Hanover, 1611, pp. 149-168.

Gianozzo Manetti, *De dignitate et excellentia hominis libri IV*, Basel, 1532.

Giovanni Pico della Mirandola, *De hominis dignitate, Opera Omnia*, Basel, 1572, vol. I, pp. 313-31.

creation than to the coldly negative Stoic tendency noted in
Salutati and in the works on *Nobility*. Indeed, as was shown,
both Burckhardt and Cassirer leaned heavily on these works
as evidence of an optimistic tendency to view this world as
beautiful, enjoyable and the handiwork of man.[81] Certainly it
is possible to find in these works statements full of appreciation
for the intellectual and physical powers with which God had
endowed man and for the delights and commodities of this
world that He had provided for man's use. There are passages
which reinforce the view that orthodox Christianity had both
its optimistic and pessimistic moments depending on whether
the greatness and majesty of the divine creation or the inferiority and corruptness of this world, especially since the Fall,
were emphasized. The two strains have been illustrated in the
writings of St. Augustine,[82] and the parallel of his enthusiastic
rhetoric with passages from these humanists will become clear
as their works are described. It remains to be seen whether such
passages are sufficient to mark their authors as optimistic or
whether they lose some of their brightness and enthusiasm
when they are placed in their full context. Even if these works
are judged optimistic, they still indicate how much the problem
of human destiny and the place of man in this world stirred
the consciousness of the humanists.

In contrast to the treatises on *Nobility*, the works on the
Dignity of Man inquire after and set forth man's position in
respect to the entire universe rather than man's earthly status
only. The crucial question to be decided is for what purpose
God created man. Bartolommeo Fazio rejected, in turn, the
view of the Platonists that God created man to dwell on earth
and contemplate the heavens, the Stoic view that man was
created for the service of man as being closer to the truth but
not enough to explain the creation, and Lactantius' view that
man was created to contemplate God. Augustine's view that

81 Burckhardt, *op. cit.,* German, pp. 281-2; trans., p. 354, see above p.
11; Cassirer, *op. cit.,* pp. 88-91, see above, p. 15.

82 See above Chapter II, especially pp. 26-29.

God, out of His immense goodness, made man for man's own sake, since God was the supreme good and since God by Himself was perfectly and entirely blessed having no need of man, is correct. To man God gave the power of reason whereby man could know, love and possess the supreme good which both is and is in God. Thus the supreme end of man is to serve God for His own sake, but this service is really to man since we can add nothing to God's divinity.[83]

Gianozzo Manetti (1396-1459), on the other hand, took the creation of man for granted as part of the creation as a whole and sought instead to answer the question why the world was created. He rejected the Democritean and Epicurean views that the world is the result of accident and the Aristotelian view that the world eternally existed. The Stoic view that the world was formed by God was closer to the truth but incomplete. He did not hesitate to assert that the world was created from nothing by omnipotent God for the sake of man. It was created, therefore, not for the sake of the world, nor for the sake of God, since this was unnecessary, but for the sake of souls, and all other animate creatures for the sake of man.[84] Thus man's excellence derives in principle from the fact that he seems to be the ultimate end or purpose of the creation.

This metaphysically grounded optimism of Fazio and Manetti, however, turned back on itself, since man, himself, has a supreme end, which is the contemplation of God and the enjoyment of this action. Thus the universe reverses, and through man, finds its end in its Creator. In the same way man was created both out of the free will of God and out of necessity because God's quality of goodness required the charity of the act of creation.[85] Although man is free to find his supreme end for himself, it necessarily has to be the contempla-

83 Fazio, *op. cit.*, p. 150.
84 Manetti, *op. cit.*, pp. 112-14.
85 Cf. A. O. Lovejoy, *The Great Chain of Being*, Cambridge, Mass., 1936, pp. 157, 315-16 for an analysis of the interplay of these two ideas in the theory of the creation.

tion and service of God. In this way the theological basis for man's dignity is at the same time a limitation upon human value and its subordination to the divine, so that the optimism of this point of view of Fazio and Manetti was susceptible of conversion into pessimism. Later citation will show how this actually happened.

Giovanni Pico della Mirandola (1463-1494) also derived man's greatness from the manner of his creation, but his theory differs from that of Fazio and Manetti. After God had created the world and had populated the heavens with eternal souls and the inferior regions with animals, He found a certain lack. No creature with power, wisdom, council and love existed. Furthermore, all the specific places in the cosmos were filled. Therefore, He decided to create man and to set him at large in the world with no particular position of his own but with the great gift of the power to occupy whatever position he willed. " I made you neither heavenly nor earthly, neither mortal nor immortal, so that you, as your own as it were free and honorable moulder and image-maker, might assume whatever form you might prefer for yourself. You can degenerate to the inferior which are beastly; you can be regenerated to the superior forms which are divine according to the desire of your mind." [86]

In this power of choosing freely what position to occupy in the universe lies the basis of man's dignity, yet with Pico also, this very latitude of choice leaves the argument open to pessimistic emphasis. On the one hand, man's freedom allows him to degenerate to lower levels and so lose his dignity, and on the other hand, man's greatest dignity necessarily lies in realizing mystical unity with God, which thus subordinates man's this-worldly potentialities to the divine end. Man's very free-

---

[86] Giovanni Pico, *op. cit.*, p. 314, " Nec te coelestem neque terrenum neque mortalem neque immortalem fecimus, ut tuiipsius quasi arbitrarius honorariusque plastes et fictor in quam malueris tute formam effingos. Poteris in inferiora quae sunt bruta degenerare. Poteris in superiora quae sunt divina ex tui animi sententia regenerari."

dom to assume whatever form he may choose enchains him to the necessities of that form. Unless man should choose higher qualities, he is degraded. Thus " whoever departs from the divine law becomes animal-like, and deservedly indeed. For bark does not make a plant, but a stupid and unfeeling nature; nor hide cattle, but a bestial and sensual soul; nor rotundity a heavenly body, but right reason; nor separation from the body an angel, but spiritual intelligence. For if you see a man crawling on the ground, given to lust, it is a beast, not a man, that you see." [87]

Pico's ethics were definitely otherworldly, for to lead a worldly life meant to abuse the liberality of God in giving man free will. Man's dignity lies, therefore, in his ability to utilize freedom as an aid to escaping this world; at the same time freedom could become an invitation to degradation. But when man is mindful of his dignity, " a certain sacred ambition comes into the soul so that, not content with mediocre things, we may draw near to the highest and (when we are able, if we will) may strive toward acquiring them with our entire powers. We should scorn the earthly, despise the heavenly [i.e. planetary and stellar realm], and from then on, forsaking whatever is of the world, hasten beyond the last mundane court to the most eminent divinity." [88].

Fazio had a similar conception of the multiple potentiality of man to find a place on higher and lower levels of existence and of the compulsion upon him to find his true excellence in the divine rather than in the earthly. " For all [forms of be-

87 *Ibid.*, p. 315, " Qui a divina lege recesserit brutum evadere et merito quidem. Neque enim plantam cortex, sed stupida et nihil sentiens natura, neque iumenta corium, sed bruta anima et sensualis, nec coelum orbiculatum corpus, sed recta ratio, nec sequestrio corporis, sed spiritualis intelligentia angelum facit. Si quem enim videris deditum ventri, humi serpentem hominem, brutum est non homo quem vides."

88 *Ibid.*, p. 316, " Invadit animum sacra quaedam ambitio, ut mediocribus non contenti anhelemus ad summa, adque (quando possumus si volumus) illa consequenda totis viribus enitamur. Dedignemur terrestia, coelestia contemnamus et quicquid mundi est denique posthabentes, ultra mundanam curiam eminentissimae divinitati proximam advolemus."

ing], witness Paul, are ours, the Highest, the Equal, the Lowest: the highest, indeed, that viewing these we might enjoy those,
in which are God and the Trinity; the equal that we might
celebrate together, in which kind are Angels to whom, although
in this life we are inferior, nevertheless, when we go to heaven
we shall be equal when, freed and relieved of earthly cares,
we give our entire selves to the contemplation and knowledge
of divinity; ours the lowest, moreover, that we may use them
for the necessary and agreeable things of life." [89] It is in the
heavenly life that man realizes his dignity. " Oh! stupidities of
the mind of men! Oh! blind cattle who, forgetful of their excellence and dignity, run with so much eagerness after this
perishable and transitory life." Some men run after pleasures;
others after riches or honors or power. " How much more
satisfying it is to embrace divine things and to meditate upon
and accustom ourselves to them while we are in this life . . ." [90]
Fazio lacks, however, the boldness and grandeur of Pico.

For Manetti too, man was able to distinguish himself from
beasts by recognizing that his dignity relates him to the divine.
Through intellectual and moral virtues he can restrain his
appetites, but if he fails to behave as a wise man, he is on the
same level as animals. Thus, while man's greatest power is
freedom, he degrades that power and loses his dignity unless
he constrains himself to live morally and contemplate the
divine.[91] Manetti, however, was far more tolerant of and fa-

89 Fazio, *op. cit.*, pp. 150-51, " Omnia enim teste Paulo nostra sunt, Summa, Aequalia, Infima. Summa quidem ut ea inspectantes his perfruamur, in
quo sunt Deus et Trinitas. Aequalia, ut convivamus, quo in genere Angeli,
quibus etsi in hac vita inferiores sumus, tamen cum in coelum emigramus,
iis pares et aequales erimus, cum terrenis curis solati et vacui totos nos
contemplationi et cognitioni divinitatis dederimus. Infima autem nostra,
ut iis ad res vitae necessarias et commodas utamur."

90 *Ibid.*, pp. 167-68, " 'O stulta hominum mentis O pectora coeca qui ex-
cellentiae ac dignitatis suae immemores, haec caduca et fluxa tanto studio
sectantur . . . Quanto autem satius esset divina amplecti et dum hac in vita
sumus illa meditari atque his assuescere . . .' "

91 Manetti, *op. cit.*, pp. 133-34, 145-57.

vorably disposed toward worldly activity and pleasure than Giovanni Pico or Fazio.

Thus, just as Salutati and the authors of treatises on *Nobility*, the authors of these works tended to locate human values outside of the field of worldly esteem. They revealed an attitude of disdain about, and a desire to escape from, the standards of prestige that prevailed in this life. The highest end of man, moreover, lay for them in spirituality, whereas for the authors of the discussions of *Nobility* human purpose was fulfilled by virtue.

Particularly with Fazio perplexity about the true place of man seemed to arise out of a feeling of bitterness and frustration from failure to snatch recognition and prestige in social relations. At one point, while detailing the delights of life in heaven in contrast with the miseries of this world, he emphasizes that in the next life there will be respect for all no matter what their station and a remarkable absence of either jealousy or contempt. " For all will not be constituted in one and the same order, but some will be superior in rank to others. Nevertheless, there will be no envy of inferiors toward a superior or of equals to an equal. For all will be content in the place assigned to them by divine justice."[92] At another place he points out that, while in this life, it is much more satisfying for man " not to make so much of these mortal affairs which among human kind always produce the greatest inequality and envy. For although in birth and death we private persons are equal to kings, yet in the middle of life, though it is very short and uncertain, we are unequal." [93]

92 Fazio, *op. cit.*, p. 163, " Neque enim omnes in uno atque eodem ordine constituentur, sed alii aliis gradu superiores erunt. Nec tamen ulla fuerit inferiorum ad superiorem aut parium ad parem invidia. Erunt enim contenti omnes loco sibi a divina iustitia designata."

93 *Ibid.*, p. 168, ". . . nec tanta haec mortalia facere, quae in humano genere inaequalitatem atque invidiam maxime semper pepererunt. Nam cum nascendi et moriendi conditione privati regibus pares sumus, media tantum vita, quae perbrevis est atque incerta, dispares sumus."

Manetti, too, felt that man's attempts to realize himself in this world led to bitter enmity, jealousy, snobbery and other harmful emotional states. "Therefore, from this so great and so sublime dignity and excellence of man, as if from the very root, envy, the exciting of displeasure, lust for domination, and ambition and other disturbances of the soul of this sort, through no wrong [i.e. naturally] arise and proceed. For whoever considers himself to have been made so worthy that he seems to be superior to and to dominate all created things, certainly will not only not suffer himself to be outstripped by others, which is the vice of envy, but rather will lust greatly to excel others, which is thought and believed to be the very vice of pride and ambition." [94] The humanists' motives for conceiving a secure, worthy man to be a spiritualized creature seeking mystical union with his Creator as in these works, or a meagerly living, virtuous sage as in the works on *Nobility,* were clearly a desire and a hope to overcome or transcend the social and material insecurities and the accompanying emotional stress of this life.

While, like Fazio and Giovanni Pico, Manetti thought that human worth was spiritual and ultimately realizable only in the next life, he, more than the others, believed that human dignity is at least partially realizable in this life as well. [95] A more just estimate of Manetti's worldliness may be gained, however, if it is viewed as occurring within the context of spirituality that has just been shown. His attitude, like St.

94 Manetti, *op. cit.,* pp. 161-62, "Ex hac igitur tanta ac tam sublimi hominis dignitate et excellentia, velut ab ipsa radice, invidia, indignatio, dominandi libido, et ambitio, atque caeterae huiusmodi animi perturbationes non iniuria oriuntur et profluunt: nam qui sese ita dignum factum fuisse considerat, ut cunctis rebus creatis praeesse ac dominari videatur, profecto non modo ab aliis superari non patietur, quod est invidiae, sed potius caeteros excellere vel maxime concupiscet, quod superbiae et ambitionis proprium vitium existimatur et creditur."

95 His treatise was placed on the Index of Pius IV, "donec emendetur." *Index Librorum Prohibitorum . . . Auctoritate Pii IIII Primum editus,* Rome 1596, p. 99. Possibly objection was taken to his sexual allusions or to his criticism of Innocent III.

Augustine's, was that man is of very great excellence because his body and, especially, his mind are endowed with partially divine powers and because so many of the goods of the world are adapted to his use and enjoyment. He devoted Book I to showing the excellence of the human body.[96] The human senses are superior to those of the beasts. The eyes can perceive color, light and form, the ears sound, tone and harmony. Through the voice and speech man can express his thoughts and communicate. The hand is wonderfully adapted for doing many things.[97] The face is shaped more for esthetic qualities than utility. The viscera and lower limbs are in their own way praiseworthy.[98] The human figure as a whole is the most noble, since it is erect rather than prone. This corresponds to the high function of man. He lacks superfluous parts such as a tail and fur and is thus set above other animals.[99]

The second book deals with the greatness of man's soul.[100] Its immortality is its most striking and most divine quality.[101] It has three natural powers: intelligence, memory and free will.[102] Through intelligence man has invented many marvellous things. The boat for example was developed by Jason. " We see the art of navigating in this way has developed little by little through many moments of time up to this our own age so that it has become even a miracle. For not only have men become accustomed daily to navigate the Brittanic and glacial ocean, as the poet said, but they recently strove to penetrate even into the interior of the Mauritanic beyond the limits previously navigable, where we have heard many cultivated and inhabited islands hitherto almost unknown were discovered." [103] Manetti

96 Manetti, *op. cit.*, pp. 16-60.   97 *Ibid.*, pp. 16-25.

98 *Ibid.*, pp. 26-40.   99 *Ibid.*, pp. 43-5.

100 *Ibid.*, pp. 61-164.   101 *Ibid.*, pp. 81-97.

102 *Ibid.*, pp. 97-109.

103 *Ibid.*, pp. 98-9, " Huiusmodi navigandi artificium paulatim per multa temporum momenta, usque ad hanc nostram aetatem ita excrevisse videmus, ut in miraculum usque processerit. Nam non modo Britannicum et glacialem oceanum, ut inquit poeta, quotidie navigare consueverunt, sed etiam in

was equally impressed with other technical and architectural wonders ranging from Noah's Ark to Brunelleschi's dome. Painters, sculptors, poets, historians, orators, jurists, philosophers, physicians, astrologers, theologians and prophets also receive their share of praise.[104] It should not be thought, however, that Manetti showed the germs of the idea of progress in his praise of human ingenuity. His examples range from the fabulous to the historical, from the ancient to the contemporary, giving no indication that he thought of an upward movement of human accomplishment through history. Further on he suggested that the reason men die younger in his days than in very early times is that the important work of building cities and founding civilization had taken place at the beginning of history so that later men have less to do.[105] His conception of history is static rather than evolutionary. The similar praise of human accomplishments seen in St. Augustine [106] shows that Manetti's enthusiasm was nothing new. Nevertheless, the allusion to the explorations of the Portuguese suggests that the age of discovery had already commenced and that awareness of it had penetrated among the Italians; it suggests the direction of human activity that in the future was going to have a profound effect on ideas and attitudes.

The third book deals with man as a whole and emphasizes particularly the works of man, the bounties of nature and the delight of heaven.[107] The purpose of Book IV is very striking, for it sets out to be a refutation of the old works on the *Misery of Human Condition* and in *Praise of Death*.[108] Since the former theme remained popular among the humanists,

intimam pene Mauritanicam, ultra terminos antea navigabiles nuper penetrare contenderunt: ubi plures cultas et habitatas insulas penitus antehac incognitas repertas fuisse audivimus."

104 *Ibid.*, pp. 99-104.
105 *Ibid.*, pp. 218-9.
106 See above, p. 28.
107 *Ibid.*, pp. 109-64.
108 *Ibid.*, pp. 165-232.

Manetti's work should indicate about how far a humanist was likely to go in the direction of worldliness. The desire to destroy the opposing argument may frequently serve as a spur to extreme statement. It should be recalled, however, that the theme of the *Dignity of Man* is not necessarily the polar opposite of the theme of the *Misery of Human Conditions,* as the co-presence of both themes in St. Augustine should prove. Indeed, Fazio stated in the introduction to the *Excellence and Dignity of Man* that he is writing the work Innocent III had intended to compose as a companion to *Contempt for the World* but failed to complete.[109]

As indicated by his citations, Manetti had in mind, as authors of the themes he intended to refute, such classical writers as the Greek Stoics and Cynics, even Aristotle, Cicero, Seneca and the elder Pliny, and such religious writers as Solomon, Job, Ambrose and Innocent III. Following Innocent III in his argument but interspersing references to the others, he first tried to prove that the mortality and weakness of the body is not natural but the result of sin. Man's partial mortality is thus his own fault and should not be lamented.[110] It cannot be denied, of course, that man suffers many bodily pains and discomforts. But so many sensual pleasures compensate for them that some pleasures even seem superfluous and evil. Man can enjoy the sight of beautiful bodies, the audition of sound and harmony, the smell of flowers, the taste of wines, the touch of soft substances. There are also such internal delights as the power to differentiate between things, imagination, thought, memory and intelligence. Man ought to enjoy and be consoled rather than suffer and lament. Man's greatest delight is *in tactu genitalium,* and more time is spent on sexual pleasure than on eating and drinking. A moderate use of the senses should bring pleasure, not labor.[111]

109 Fazio, *op. cit.,* p. 149.

110 Manetti, *op. cit.,* pp. 186-7.

111 *Ibid.,* pp. 188-92. Innocent III, *op. cit.,* Lib. I. cap. i, " De miserabili humanae conditionis ingressu."

Even though the body of the first man had been made of mud, the human body is still marvelous and superior. Winds, planets and stars are made of the higher elements, air and fire, but still are not sensitive and animate. Man is greater than all other creatures both animate and inanimate, for unless he sins he cannot die.[112] There is nothing degrading about conception and pregnancy, for human sperm and blood come from superfluous foods and, since the human diet is more delicate, are purer and better than those of animals.[113]

Against those who emphasized the lowliness of the mind, Manetti alleged that the mind's origins and powers are not earthly, since memory, thought and foresight can come only from God. As Aristotle claimed, the mind is composed of a fifth element which is above the other four.[114] The soul, of course, suffers many agonies, yet even this is a mark of human superiority, since a stone cannot even suffer.[115] The " praise of death " is no criticism of life, since death is anticipated in the hope of even greater immortal life.[116]

Manetti paused to devote some space to refuting Solomon by showing his self-contradictions, [117] and then returned to his chief antagonist, Innocent III. His next point against Innocent was that he erred in deriving the name *Eva* from *heu*, " alas," and in trying in this way to show that men had been miserable from the very start. Jerome has shown that *Eva* derived from " mother of men." If Innocent was wrong here, he must be subject to error elsewhere.[118] It was Innocent's claim

112 Manetti, *op. cit.*, pp. 193-4. Innocent III, *op. cit.*, Lib. I, cap. 2, " De vilitate materiae ipsius hominis."

113 Manetti, *op. cit.*, p. 195. Innocent III, *op. cit.*, Lib. I, caps. 3, 4, 5, " Divisio conceptionis ", " De conceptione infantis ", " Quali cibo conceptus nutriatur in utero."

114 Manetti, *op. cit.*, pp. 196-8. Innocent III, *op. cit.*, Lib. I, cap. 6, " De imbecillitate infantis."

115 Manetti, *op. cit.*, p. 202.

116 *Ibid.*, p. 203.   117 *Ibid.*, pp. 206-07.

118 *Ibid.*, pp. 209-14. Innocent III, *op. cit.*, Lib. I, cap. 7, " De dotore partus et ejulatu infantis."

that man is miserable and contemptible because of the naked-
ness of man's body.[119] " To this we reply that it was necessary
for men to be thus born for the sake of comeliness and beauty.
For in the first place, if we were born covered and enveloped
with various and diverse hides after the fashion of beasts, it
could not sufficiently be said or stated how filthy and how ugly
that aspect would be. Also on account of the excellence of our
composition, which grows out of the delights of human semen,
it could not happen and come about otherwise; but if it could
have happened otherwise, certainly nature would never have
hidden away in strange garments the human body, the most
beautiful of all her works and indeed the most handsome article
marvelously fashioned by her, lest perchance [she should have
hidden away] its beauties in incongruous and reproachful clothing." [120]

Against Innocent's comparison of the fruits of men and
trees,[121] Manetti claimed that human fruits contribute greatly
to knowledge and action. Spittle is used to cure serpent bite,
urine to loosen the bowels and to conserve the vision, excrement
to fertilise fields.[122] On the discomforts of old age and the
brevity of life.[123] Manetti argued, as was shown above, that
pleasures make up for the discomforts and that men no longer
need to live as long as before the time of Moses when the race

119 Innocent III, *op. cit.*, Lib. I, cap. 8, " De nuditate hominis."

120 Manetti, *op. cit.*, pp. 214-15, " Ad quod nos decoris et pulchritudinis
causa homines ita nasci oportuisse respondemus. Primo nanque si variis
diversisque pellibus instar brutorum cooperti et induti nasceremur, quam
turpis et quam foedus esset aspectus ille, satis dici explicarive non posset.
Ob excellentiam quoque complexionis nostrae quae ex deliciis humani
seminis procedebat, aliter contingere et evenire non poterat: sed quando
aliter fieri potuisset, profecto natura quae humanum corpus caeter-
orum omnium operum suorum pulcherrimum ac nimirum formosissimum
opificium ab ea mirabiliter fabrefactum, nunquam alieno indumento abscond-
isset, ne forte pulchritudines suas incongruis et objectis velaminibus."

121 Innocent III, *op. cit.*, Lib. I, cap. 9, " Quem fructu homo producit."

122 Manetti, *op. cit.*, pp. 216-17.

123 Innocent III, *op. cit.*, Lib. I, caps. 10, 11, " De incommodis senectutis
et brevitate vitae hominis ", " De incommodis senectutis."

had to be propagated, cities built, and arts and sciences created.[124] Labor is necessary in life,[125] but it is the means to pleasure; the two are inseparable.[126] As for the various cares and anxieties of men,[127] after the resurrection they will disappear.[128]

This last argument was typical of the limitation of other-worldliness on Manetti's view. His argument seems to boil down to the claim that most of the circumstances which seemed to make human life miserable were compensated for by pleasures in this world or by delights in heaven. He did not claim that this life was a completely happy one. He was only partially worldly, for he saw many evil features in this life and many advantages over this life in the resurrection. There man will enjoy eternal health, eternal youth, a light and subtle body free of necessities, beauty without blemish, immortality, constant repose, and perpetual joy. The glories of heaven will be shown to man by Christ Himself.[129] Manetti still further limited his argument by requiring virtue of man while he is in this life if he wanted to benefit in the next life. The alternative was sinning and then suffering eternal damnation which he described at length.[130] He ended his treatise with an exhortation to men to be virtuous and realize their dignity and excellence so they might ultimately enjoy the pleasures of heaven.[131]

Manetti's point of view was ambiguous. On the one hand, he differed from a definitely pessimistic writer such as Innocent III. In contrast to the old theme of contempt for man, Manetti admired the beauty, complexity and aptness of the

124 Manetti, *op. cit.*, pp. 218-20.

125 Innocent III, *op. cit.*, Lib. I, cap. 12, "De labore mortalium."

126 Manetti, *op. cit.*, pp. 220-21.

127 Innocent III, *op. cit.*, Lib. I, caps. 13, 14, 15, "De studio sapientum", "De variis studiis hominum", "De diversis anxietatibus."

128 Manetti, *op. cit.*, p. 222.

129 *Ibid.*, pp. 223-27.

130 *Ibid.*, pp. 229-31.

131 *Ibid.*, p. 232.

human body and mind, and he praised the works of man. On the other hand, he admitted that much of the criticism that had been made about human conditions was true. Man, however, was foolish to spend his time worrying about these miseries. He should instead count what pleasures he enjoyed as blessings and place his hope in gaining eternal bliss in heaven through living virtuously.

Manetti was very much like St. Augustine in all this. But he went farther and treated the pleasures of this world as values to be sought almost for their own sake, whereas St. Augustine recognized these pleasures only as signs of the greatness of the work of the Creator. Yet Manetti did not go so far as to approve the distorted extremes of Epicureanism, for he counted some pleasures as superfluous and harmful. He differed further from St. Augustine in that for him the heavily accented side of the picture was the favorable one, while for St. Augustine the miseries weighed more heavily.

Manetti's work on the *Dignity and Excellence of Man,* therefore, shows that he had a favorable view of this life, althought only slightly more than St. Augustine. Optimistic as this work is, it still remains good evidence of how much the humanists were pressed to seek the purpose of human life and explain the problem of human destiny and conditions. It is evidence of an uncertain and doubtful disposition which in less confident writers grew as readily into pessimism as into optimism. This work, in spite of its optimism, suggests the likelihood of a humanist becoming a pessimist. A few shades of emphasis in the other direction and Manetti too would have been one.[132]

132 It is probably of some significance in this connection that, if it is true, as Vespasiano da Bisticci alleged, Manetti wrote this work at the very height of his career while he was Vicar of Scarperia. Shortly afterwards Manetti suffered the super-tax of (according to Vespasiano) 166,000 gold florins, which completely ruined him. Thereafter he lived as an exile at the courts of Nicolas V in Rome and Alfonso in Naples. (Vespasiano da Bisticci, *Viti di uomini illustri del secolo XV,* English translation by W. G. & E. Waters as *The Vespasiano Memoirs,* London, 1926, pp. 390-95.) Vespasiano's chronology and figures were apt to be inaccurate, but he knew

The preoccupation of the humanists with thoughts about prestige and how it was to be attained, as the attitude of Salutati and the authors of works on *Nobility* and on the *Dignity of Man* showed, was an indication of discontent on their part with an ordinary everyday life in society and of a desire both to escape from the hum-drum and instability of ordinary life and to justify their aloofness from it. In some cases their discontent had material grounds, for some of them suffered from lack and uncertainty of reward. According to Baron [133] this explained the idealization of a life of poverty by the fourteenth century humanists. In other cases there must have been other grounds for the attitude of withdrawal from ordinary life which Baron's explanation does not comprehend,[134] for poverty was praised by many humanists, especially of the fifteenth century, who had positions yielding substantial material rewards. Discontent for such men could not have material but may have had social or psychological grounds. In the former cases aloofness from worldly standards of pres-

Manetti better than most persons he wrote about. Perhaps, if Manetti had postponed writing this work for a few years, his attitude would have been different.

Manetti was one of the Florentine citizen-humanists whom Baron, *op. cit.*, p. 18, described as being "at home in the world of active life and earthly goods." Baron did not mention this work of Manetti, however, and based his conclusions about him on his funeral oration on the death of Leonardo Bruni where Bruni's thrift and ambition were praised, and on Manetti's life of Boccaccio where it was claimed that poverty was a great obstacle to virtue for Boccaccio. *Ibid.*, pp. 20, 22.

133 Baron, *op. cit.*, p. 12, "The social position of the humanists during this period fostered such views. Humanism had not yet found its place in Renaissance society. Its exponents were for the most part vagrant teachers or secretaries . . . They found the sole justification for their existence in the ideal of the wise man's independence of social position and material possessions."

134 Baron admitted there were other cases, *Ibid.*, p. 26, "The pride of acquisition by one's own efforts, which was the background for the civic championship of the good things of life, was lacking in the case of courtiers and humanistic literati." But he failed to offer any convincing explanation of the survival of the fourteenth century attitude in such figures as Poggio, Fazio or Platina.

tige was involuntary, and the idealization of poverty a rationalization of their own meager circumstances. In the latter cases withdrawal into a life of virtuous or pious study was voluntary, or at least the idealization of it was, for it may not have been carried out in practice. Such a withdrawal may have been a pose assumed to induce self-respect and to give a sense of ultimate purpose and moral value to the practice of humanism. Whatever a plausible explanation of it might be, it is indisputable that it was a pose assumed by many.

The significant thing about the attempts of the humanists to find an ultimate purpose for their lives is that the answer was frequently found in a rejection of worldly standards and a substitution of ascetic or otherworldly moral or religious standards. As such it indicates a doubtful attitude toward man's condition in this life. It involved at the same time a feeling that a person, such as a humanist, who subordinated his worldly desires to ascetic or otherworldly ends was a superior or a more truly human person. In this sense it gave rise to an intellectual snobbishness and an aristocratic attitude that ran parallel to the expressions of conceit and the exaggerated self-praise of the humanists, and to their unhistorical conception of their own place in the history of culture as the " restorers of learning." On the other hand, it can not be doubted that for some writers man could achieve a very exalted place in the universe albeit this was a consequence of his spiritual powers.

CHAPTER IV

THEORIES OF MAN AND HIS FITNESS FOR HAPPINESS

WHEREAS the previous chapter discussed the views of the humanists on life in general, this chapter will attempt to analyze their theories about the constitution of individual man with reference to its advantages and disadvantages in bringing happiness to him in this life. From the general question of human life, it goes to the specific phase of man's nature. There is inevitably a certain amount of overlapping between the two chapters, since a discussion of life purposes involves theories about the nature of man, and, conversely, a conception of man's composition will take shape according to how well man is thought to be fitted for pursuing what were assumed to be his ultimate ends.

Probably all humanists thought of the individual as being made up of material and spiritual parts. Man, of course, had a body and a soul. In some cases the body was conceived to be a sort of shell or garment for the soul, which was in turn divided into separate parts. In these views the body was comparatively neutral with regard to the soul, merely placing certain obstacles in the way of the activities which resided in the soul. The real problem of the fitness of man's nature for happiness involved the ability of the different parts of the soul to function in relation to each other rather than the relations of the soul with its body. The soul was usually thought of as being divided into the feelings and the reason, with the addition in some cases of a third part, the intellect. In other cases a simple distinction between the body and the soul, each having certain qualities of its own which might be in conflict or in harmony with the other, was considered sufficient to explain man's nature.

The majority of the humanists held a theory within the first, more psychologically elaborate conception of man's nature as made up of a relatively neutral body and a soul divided into two or more parts having various possible relationships. Within this group were the humanists whose ideas showed Stoic and Christian ascetic, Neoplatonic and Christian otherworldly, and Aristotelian tendencies, although it was quite possible for a humanist to take a mixed position. Some humanists were likely to think that happiness depended on the relations between the sentient and rational parts of the soul, exclusive of the intellect. The feelings and the reason might be thought to be in permanent and necessary conflict, the inevitable tendency of the feelings being toward experience of passions resulting in sin, which could be avoided only by the coercion and repression of the passions by reason resulting in virtue. Both Christian asceticism and Stoicism had this conception of man's nature, although they explained it differently. In the case of the former the victory of reason was achieved only through the mediation of divine grace; in the latter it could be gained only by the very few and very wise men. In general it was a harsh estimate of humanity. The humanists whose ideas followed these tendencies will be analyzed first.

A variant of this theory held that the feelings and reason were in conflict, that the emotions led to vice, which was miserable, that reason led to virtue, but that complete victory bringing happiness was impossible in this life. Man's happiness depended on the achievement of a spiritual state through the exercise of the intellect in the contemplation of God. This was the otherworldly Christian and Neoplatonic point of view. A third variant of this theory conceived of reason as acting as a mediator between the propensities of the passions to move to one extreme of feeling or another. The moderation in the experience of emotion thus established corresponded to some virtue lying between two opposite vices such as liberality between avarice and prodigality. The body played a modifying role of making the habit of virtue more easy to acquire if the wants of the body were well satisfied and more difficult if the body were in lack. This was the Aristotelian theory of happiness. It was founded on a conception of harmony between the feelings and reason with the relative neutrality of body and intellect. It was comparatively optimistic, since it was believed that man was capable of a harmonious internal adjustment provided external conditions of life were favorable.

The simple conception of man as divided into a corporeal and a spiritual part was very infrequent among the humanists. It logically might have been held in any of four possible sub-positions: that matter and spirit were in irresolvable conflict, that they existed together in comparative harmony, that complete victory of the spirit over the body was possible, and that the soul was really a mere front or disguise for the body. The first sub-position was the theory of the Gnostics and Manicheans. Earthly happiness was obviously impossible for it. It is interesting, but in view of its unsavory reputation not surprising, that no humanist could be found holding to it. The second sub-position held that the desires of both soul and body might be gratified. It was comparatively optimistic, although the demands of soul and body might at some points be mutually exclusive and thus reduce man's composure. Epicureanism generally fell within this theory; Lorenzo Valla, whose ideas will be considered below, defended this theory against some of its perversions. The third sub-position held it possible for man to be released from his bodily demand. It was mystical and spiritual, also rare among humanists. The nearest approach to it was the Neoplatonist view that man could rise above the demands of this life through the intellect. The fourth sub-position may have been held by some of the humanists, but because of its obvious materialism was not likely to be admitted. This was the form which the corruption of Epicureanism, ascribed to Antonio Panormità by Valla in the second book of *De Voluptate,* assumed. The views set forth under this group, because of their closeness to the Aristotelian theory, will be considered in conjunction with it.

Other possible theories of man and happiness might be worked out and outlined which seem to have been lacking among the humanists, such as the view that happiness came through human achievement and hard work, or that it came from amicable relations with other men. The theories that they held definitely mark the humanists for what they were—writers who held themselves aloof from their fellow men and who tended to avoid the practical issues of living. This is suggested by the similarity of the different theories that they did hold. With the single exception of the extreme form of vulgar Epicureanism, which perverted the moderation of the original doctrine into a belief that all gratification was bodily even when it seemed to be spiritual, all of them considered that the desire to gratify either bodily wants or the senses had to be suppressed, or at least limited.

This indicates a negative attitude about the means of gratifying the desires and suggests that the humanists felt that the conditions of the world made it extremely difficult for man to make a direct happy adjustment with nature and that any direct adjustment with the environment was uncertain, arbitrary and temporary. Complete satisfaction with life was therefore out of the question with any of the theories. A man was not conceived to be an integrated being, capable of making a direct relationship with nature in solution of his wants and desires. Instead, all of these theories conceived of man as being compelled to make an internal adjustment. Man's nature was viewed dualistically, and it was necessary for his different parts to be in harmony with each other in order either to avoid the insecurity of the difficulty of making an external adjustment or to supplement whatever external adjustment might be made. Too much should not be asked of the humanists, of course, and, considering that there was a large amount of justice in their grave view of the outer world (as the next chapter will show), they must be granted the appropriateness of their psychological approach to the problem of happiness.

A corollary of the feeling that the conditions of the world were unfavorable, implied in the emphasis laid on an internal adjustment, was that man as he faced the world was too fragile, too involved in making an internal adjustment and

too corrupt to be able to make a successful external adjustment in defiance of the evil and insecurity of the world, without divine intervention or the aid of magic or miracle. This
attitude did not, however, necessarily follow from every theory
about the nature of man. It was a part of only those theories
which held that satisfactory external adjustment was out of
the question and that only the conquest of the feelings by
reason, extremely difficult as it was, brought any sort of tranquillity. The more optimistic theories held that a less rigorous
internal adjustment was a relatively easy supplement to an
external adjustment that was insufficient by itself but con-
tributory to happiness. For difficult and miserable as the conditions of human life were, they were not completely lacking
in compensations.[1] It is significant here, however, that this
distinctly negative feeling about man, characteristic of such
medieval writings as Innocent III's *Contempt for the World,*
found continuators among the humanists. Samples of this attitude will make a good beginning for a description of the
theories of the more rigoristic group which held that reason
and emotion were in conflict.

Petrarch's conceptions of human nature place him definitely
among the dour Stoic group. Petrarch considered St. Augustine
his special spiritual guide and master, and like him he in no
way definitely committed himself on the side of confidence in
human powers to cope with the difficulties of life in this world.
He felt at times that with the help of leisure, pleasant rural
surroundings, the song of birds, and fine literature he could
achieve a contentment and serenity in life which the turmoil
and mad struggle for wealth and position in the city made
impossible.[2] Yet even in this mood he revealed a profound
doubt about the chances of most men to gain this calm and
detachment. " For man," he wrote, " is not only a base and
unclean animal, but furthermore . . . he is pernicious, unstable,

1 *Cf. e. g.* Manetti, above, p. 73.
2 *Cf. De vita solitaria,* Eng. trans. by Jacob Zeitlin, Urbana, 1924.

faithless, inconstant, fierce and bloody, unless by the rare grace of God he puts off his bestiality and puts on humanity, unless, in short, he learns to make himself a man out of a common creature." [3]

At other times Petrarch felt that material comforts were necessary for any sort of happiness in this life. Toward the end of his life he came more and more to the position that wealth and poverty made little difference and that all depended on an internal solution. But throughout his life he was torn back and forth in different directions, now trusting, now doubting, always seeking, and rarely finding security. [4]

Probably Petrarch's strongest statements on the difficulties facing man in resolving the inner conflicts between his reason and his emotions occur in his *Secret Conflict of My Desires*. [5] At great length he reviewed the passions which had impelled him toward one false goal after another and the struggles he went through to conquer the longings of his lower nature. He made St. Augustine the spokesman for his better self and over and over again he chides, admonishes and advises himself through the mouth of the saint. At one point he complains about the difficulties he has experienced in trying to achieve his ambition of gaining recognition from the world. St. Augustine sought to answer his complaint by depicting the miserable state of man which should make him realize that only by making the supreme effort to suppress his desires could he avoid the very depths of sorrow. " Behold him naked and unformed, born in wailings and tears, comforted with a few drops of milk, trembling and crawling, needing the hand of another, fed and clothed from the beasts of the field, his body feeble, his spirit restless, subject to all kinds of sickness, the prey of passions innumerable, devoid of all reason, joyful today, tomorrow sorrowful, in both full of agitation, incapable of mastering himself, unable to restrain his appetite, . . . at once greedy and

3 *Ibid.,* p. 101.

4 See Baron, *op. cit.,* pp. 6-12 for a sketch of Petrarch's quest for security.

5 *Op. cit.*

timid, disgusted with what he has, longing after what he has lost, discontented alike with past, present and future, full of pride in his misery, and aware of his frailty, baser than the vilest worms, his life is short, his days uncertain, his fate inevitable since Death in a thousand forms is waiting for him at last." [6]

This picture of the complete unfitness of man to cope with the world shows how the trouble with man, to this way of thinking, was his weakness in the face of nature. That is why it was a sign of disgrace that man is " the prey of passions innumerable, devoid of all reason." If man were well fit to cope with nature and fortune, he might well follow his desires; unfortunately he is not. Petrarch says as much when a little later he has St. Augustine admonish him to, " Give up, there-fore, your dreams of the impossible, and be content to accept the lot of humanity." Poor man is only able to strive to sup-press his desires. He cannot " shake off the yoke of fortune that presses even on kings." He can gain tranquility only when, " caring not a straw for human passions," he brings himself with the aid of reason under " the rule of virtue." [7] Petrarch's view of man was sad indeed, for he saw man faced with the grim choice of following his passions and being frustrated at every turn or going through the agonizing struggle revealed in this treatise of trying to enforce the rule of reason over the passions of the soul. Freedom from conflict, if achieved at all, could be bought only at the price of foregoing the pleasures of the senses and the psychological rewards of prestige and recognition by the world that he desired.

Coluccio Salutati has already been shown to have had a very rigorous ideal of life. [8] To him the virtue which marked off the learned from the mass of men was achieved through the suppression of feeling by the reason. The difficulties of achieving security and prestige through the ordinary activities

6 *Ibid.*, pp. 70-1.

7 *Ibid.*, pp. 71, 72.

8 See above, pp. 57-59.

of men led him to turn aside from that path and idealize the very admission of his defeat by the world and society.[9] The difficulties of the world as a field of human activity were described by him especially in *De saeculo et religione*.[10] He berates himself at many points in this work for his foolish belief that he could satisfy his desires in the world. " Woe is me, woe is me, You have made the ways of life known to me Lord; I moreover, am corrupt and I am made abominable in my desires." [11] " We, stupid and mad, strive to be happy nevertheless in the world, and, what is more inane, we believe and boast that we are blessed and happy among these mundane, false and perishable things." [12] Man is no better than the beasts if he cannot conquer his passions and turn away from worldly desires.[13] Indeed, " the soul enters as if by five gates into knowledge of corporal things, whence we are drawn into vices unless the mind is stirred by better reason. These are the five senses." [14]

Poggio Bracciolini, as his treatise on *Nobility* has shown,[15] also belonged with those who conceived of human nature as involved in a perpetual warfare between the reason and the emotions. In his treatise on *The Misery of Human Condition*,[16]

9 *Op. cit.*

10 Coluccio Salutati, *De saeculo et religione*, Cod. Laur. Plut. 53, 4, fol. 260 ff. Analyzed in Alfred von Martin, *Mittelalterliche Welt- und Lebensanschauung in Spiegel der Schriften Coluccio Salutatis*, Munich and Berlin, 1913. MS. cited by Baron, *op. cit.*, p. 16.

11 *Ibid.*, fol. 279r, cited von Martin, p. 45, ". . . heu miser, heu miser, notas fecisti michi domine vias vite, ego autem corruptus sum et factus sum abominabilis in studiis meis . . ."

12 *Ibid.*, fol. 272 v, cited von Martin, p. 55, ". . . nitimur tamen in mundo, stulti atque dementes, esse nos beatos, quod inanius est, inter haec mundana, falsa atque caduca nos beatos ac felices credimus et iactamus."

13 Cited von Martin, p. 40 from letter to Francesco Bruni, *Epist.*, ed. Novati, I, 263 ff.

14 *Ibid.*, p. 265, cited von Martin, p. 41, " quinque quasi ostiis in noticiam corporalium anima se extendit, unde in vitia trahimur, nisi mens meliore ratione agatur. hec sunt quinque illi sensus."

15 See above, pp. 53-56.

16 *Op. cit.*

written toward the end of his career,[17] he remained faithful to the ideas he had earlier expressed. This work was devoted to proving two points. First, human nature was so helpless in the face of the evil conditions of the world that it was forced almost universally to suffer continued frustration of every desire for any sort of security, well-being or prestige. Only in extremely rare cases a man with unusual power of reason through divine grace was able to repress his passions and find some small amount of peace in this life. Second, nature and fortune seemed peculiarly adapted to making man miserable. Against the argument of a participant in the debate that it is only the stupid and ignorant who are unable to gain security and position for themselves Poggio replied, " You declare that reason has been given to us by which the powers of fortune are weakened; I admit that is true in what concerns the soul, if anyone could freely use it, but very many obstacles and difficult hazards have been opposed to acquiring virtue . . . For avarice, prodigality, luxury, fear, rashness, lust, envy, pride, ambition and six hundred adverse disturbances of the soul, powerful and most disturbing to reason, make war against and sharply pursue reason; few have hitherto been found who conquered their force [i.e. of the passions] by reason." [18] No one is exempt from these passions. " Therefore it must be conceded that since all are evil, they are also miserable." [19]

17 Cf. Ernst Walser, *Poggius Florentinus Leben und Werke*, Leipzig and Berlin, 1914, p. 305. Walser dates this work 1455. The supposed dialogue at the bedside of Cosimo de' Medici must have taken place in 1453 from the reference to the fall of Constantinople and to Poggio's age as 72.

18 *De miseria*, p. 92, ". . . datum nobis rationem asseris, qua fortunae vires debilarentur, fateor id verum esse quo ad animum spectat, si quis illa libere uti posset, sed plurima obstacula et tanquam duri obices oppositi sunt ad consequendam virtutem... Bellantur enim atque acriter rationem persequuntur avaritia, prodigalitas, luxuria, metus, temeritas, libido, aemulatio, superbia, ambitio et sexcentae perturbationes animi adversae, validae atque infestissimae rationi, quarum vim pauci sunt adhuc reperti, qui ratione superarent."

19 *Ibid.*, p. 93, " Ergo concedatur oportet quoniam mali sint omnes, miseros quoque esse."

It can be seen that on this question, just as on the problem of nobility,[20] Poggio was inclined to take a more radical position than other writers, and to assert that there was no way of making an adjustment externally or internally. When he was again opposed by the argument that in view of the existence past and present of some happy men, " therefore this your miserable condition of life does not rule all men but rather comprehends the stupid and ignorant and uneducated crowd which, made in the manner of cattle without reason, without prudence, without virtue, is moved only by emotion and some spontaneous and sudden impulse," [21] the force of this assertion led him finally to modify his view to that more usually held. " I do not say this about the misery of one or another person, Cosimo, but I am speaking about the common misery of man's lot. I know that certain persons can be excepted from this destiny of miseries, because the kindness of God made them greater in virtue than the rest, but they are rarer than black swans and white crows, as the saying goes." [22]

Poggio also thought that the necessity for man, in the few cases where it is possible, to gain security by an inner rather than an outer solution, comes from the natural weakness of man in trying to cope with the world. After detailing in a long passage [23] the miseries that men go through in trying to find an adequate place in the world and the unfavorable conditions of nature and society, he concluded that " we have been abandoned to so many calamities, so many weapons of fortune, so

20 See above, p. 54 where Poggio first denies that any kind of nobility is genuine and then modifies his position.

21 *De miseria,* p. 95, " Non igitur omnibus hominibus haec tua imperat miseria conditio vitae, sed stultos tantum atque ignavium et imperitum comprehendit vulgus, quod nulla ratione, nulla prudentia, nulla virtute factum more pecudum solo movetur sensu impetuque voluntario quodam atque repentino."

22 *Idem.* " Hic ego non de unius inquam, aut alterius Cosme, sed de communi conditionis humanae miseria · sum locutus. Scio quosdam excipi posse ab hac miseriarum sorte, quod Dei pietas reliquis insigniores virtute fecit, sed sunt nigris cignis et cornis albis, ut dicitur, rariores."

23 *Ibid.,* pp. 104-8.

many temporal vicissitudes that the condition of weakness given to us seems very hard to bear." [24] In the preface to this work he specifically states that his motive in writing is to recommend an inner conquest of security as a substitute for a struggle with the external environment which could only bring misery. " No writers seem to me to have contributed more fittingly to human welfare than those who have devoted their energies to coercing excessive desires of the soul as well as to restraining ambition and superfluous appetite for the goods of fortune, dangerous evils to mortals. For those who reveal the miserable condition of this life to readers and teach that all our miseries arise from the goods of fortune and that, therefore, a limit is to be set to desires, are indeed those who deserve most from humanity." [25] But it was a small comfort to offer as a substitute for the miserable struggle with the world the equally arduous task of repressing one's desires, which Poggio, himself, admitted could only be accomplished rarely and with the aid of God.

It was probably more than coincidence that another of the humanists, whose works on true nobility have been analyzed, should write on the need to introvert one's struggle with the outside world, for a most pressing desire that was not easily satisfied by a man of letters was the craving for social distinction. Platina's *Dialogues on False and True Good*,[26] like Petrarch's *Secret,* gives a picture of Platina's own struggle against his passionate longing for well-being and affluence.

---

24 *Ibid.,* p. 108, " Tot enim rerum casibus, tot fortunae telis, tot varietatibus temporum addicti sumus, ut durissima nobis videatur data conditio infirmitatis."

25 *Ibid.,* p. 86, ". . . nulli mihi proprius ad hominum utilitatem accessisse videntur, quam hi qui ad coercendas nimias animi cupiditates, tum etiam ad referendum ambitionem, supervacaneumque rerum fortuitarum appetitum perniciosa mortalibus mala suam operam contulerunt. Nam qui huius vite miseram conditionem legentibus exponunt docentque nostras miserias omnes a fortunae bonis proficisci, ideoque modum statuendum esse cupiditatibus, hi sunt profecto qui plurimum de humano genere mereantur."

26 *Op. cit.*

It consists of three dialogues between Platina and three successive visitors to his cell during his imprisonment by Paul II.
Although Platina was stubborn in his argument that only by
gaining material prosperity and comfort could he live without
misery, he finally admitted, " having been convinced by the
best reasons that the supreme happiness is in God which no
one could ever attain unless by scorning the goods of fortune
and repressing all cupidities and perturbations, he should have
abandoned himself to the contemplation of divine things." [27]
This was after he had been told that his own miseries were
small compared to those of many other men, that fortitude is
the proper and natural attitude for man to assume,[28] that man
is made of the four elements and a fifth essence—intelligence—
and that the only way man can be distinguished from other
animals is by using reason to repress his desires.[29] It is true
that men are born for labors and not for delights,[30] if they
live virtuously and not like beasts, and that " this imposes
vigilance, heat, cold, thirst, hunger, continence, integrity and
almost infinite hardships on us," [31] but it brings freedom from
frustration. When Platina complained that " I have no patrimony, . . . no private funds, no home, no household goods,"
and that " money is so honored in our age that he is held
eccentric who spurning the goods of fortune abandons himself to virtue and knowledge of things: all despise, avoid, spit
upon him as a wicked fanatic," [32] it was pointed out that those

27 *Ibid.*, p. 22, " optimis rationibus victus, summam felicitatem in deo esse:
quam adipisci nemo unquam poterit, nisi spretis fortunae bonis, repressisque
cupiditatibus omnibus et perturbationibus, contemplatione rerum divinarum
sese addixerit."

28 *Ibid.*, pp. 3-4.

29 *Ibid.*, pp. 6-7.

30 *Ibid.*, p. 15.

31 *Ibid.*, p. 11, " Haec nobis vigilias, aestus, frigora, sitim, famem, con-
tinentiam, integritatem et labores fere infinitos proponit . . ."

32 *Ibid.*, p. 17, " Nullum est mihi patrimonium . . . nulla privata pecunia,
non domus, non suppellex . . . tanto enim aetate nostra pecunia in honore
sunt, ut pro monstra habeatur, qui spretis fortunae bonis, virtuti se et

who pursue wealth are miserable and that the poor man's lot has some advantages.[33]

The conception of human nature as consisting of the feelings whose passions carried man into misery, and of the reason with which man could suppress his passions and become virtuous, was held by other humanists whose theories will shortly be examined. Whereas they believed that human happiness depended on other things than the outcome of this conflict alone, Petrarch, Salutati, Poggio and Platina relied primarily on the strength of human reason to enforce order and tranquillity upon the disturbed soul of man and belong, therefore, to a separate group. Nothing but misery was seen in the attempt to gratify human desires in an active life. This does not mean that they denied that some sort of worldly activity at least was necessary, but that they felt that no good could come to man from it. Their attitude toward man led them to favor the teachings of the Stoics, who relied, as St. Augustine charged,[34] on the power of reason alone to achieve contentment.

The second group of humanists, like St. Augustine, differed from those who relied on reason and were closer to his views in believing that virtue, or the suppression of passion by reason, was merely a means toward salvation, which could come only in the next life. They were therefore more sweeping in their rebuke of this life than the humanists of Stoic tendency, since a life devoted to learning, virtue or contemplation could no more bring security and happiness, as compared with the life to come, than a life of sensual gratification. And as they did not place an active life far below the life of the impecunious sage, they were frequently more appreciative of the gift of sensual pleasure that the Creator had provided for man than those who emphasized the conflict of reason and passion. Their

cognitioni rerum addixerit: hunc ut phanaticum, ut prophanum contemnunt, devitant, inspuunt omnes."

33 *Ibid.*, pp. 17-18.
34 See above, p. 24.

doubt about this world was a function of their Christian expectancy about the next world.

A rigid distinction between the two points of view, however, cannot be maintained, for the Stoicizing humanists differed among themselves in the degree to which they felt that repression of the desires by reason brought contentment. Petrarch probably went as far as any of them in believing that the "solitary life" freed man from the miseries of the world.[35] Salutati also always held in theory that the contemplative life was superior to the active, but he was never able completely to put down his longings for fame and material rewards.[36] Platina regarded virtue and the suppression of cupidity as the means to happiness rather than happiness itself. This required the addition of contemplation of divine things.[37] Poggio, however, wanted to conclude that no man could be happy and admitted that a few might be only under pressure of argument.[38] He came closer to the position of St. Augustine in recognizing the misery not only of a sensual life but of the struggle to put down the passions. In talking of the religious orders, Poggio argued that the religious could not be considered happier than other men since they were subject to all the conditions of human life.[39] He thus repudiated the partial tolerance of "rationalism" which had from time to time cropped up to claim that a religious life brought greater happiness in this world. In the similarity of point of view of the Stoicizing humanists to monasticism, which von Martin's study of Salutati showed, there was, moreover, a parallel in the tendency to find partial salvation in this world for a small elite living according to a strict regime as well as in the tendency to reject worldly values.

35 See above, p. 85.
36 See above, pp. 57-61 and von Martin II, pp. 155 ff.
37 See above, pp. 90-91 and *De Falso et vero bono*, pp. 21, 22.
38 See above, pp. 88-89.
39 *De miseria* etc., p. 101.

Bartolommeo Fazio, as has already been shown from his treatise on the *Dignity of Man,* relied on contemplation of divine things to enable man ultimately to escape from insecurity and considered that this solution of man's difficulties was possible only in the next world.[40] He showed in the same work that it was the difficulty of making an external adjustment in this world that led him to seek something better. " For how could they [worldly values] delight man if he knew that all his goods will perish along with this short and uncertain life? "[41] And when men achieve happiness in the next life the contrast with this world will have increased their pleasure. " Nor will that joy of the blessed have been mediocre, since they will think from what very great discomforts, what innumerable dangers, what various calamities, in which this most miserable life which we so greatly desire abounds, they have been snatched away."[42] In an earlier work on *Human Happiness*[43] he had specifically discussed the problem of the conditions of this life. His definition of happiness showed that he had nothing against man's finding comfort and security in this world provided that the world could have been a favorable environment in which " to have abundance and refinement in all those things which are necessary and proper for nourishing and adorning the body, to be content with the present condition of things, to feel that nothing is lacking, to desire nothing, to aim at no advantage, finally to lack all anxiety of mind, all discomfort of body."[44] But unfortunately, he felt

40 See above, pp. 67-68.

41 *De excellentia et praestantia hominis, op. cit.,* p. 159, "Quid enim ea hominem delectare possent, si sciret omnia eius bona una cum ipsa vita brevi atque incerta interitura esse? "

42 *Ibid.,* p. 166, " Nec illa fuerit beatorum mediocris laetitia cum cogitabunt quam maximis molestis, quam innumerabilibus periculis, quam variis calamitatibus erepti fuerint, quibus haec miserrima vita, quam tantopere cupimus, redundat."

43 *De viri felicitate, seu summi boni fruitione,* Leyden, 1628. Also printed as *De vitae felicitate* in *Dialogi decem variorum auctorum,* s.l., 1473. Described by Thorndike, *op. cit.,* pp. 185-87.

44 *Ibid.,* (Leyden edition) p. 29, "habere earum rerum omnium copiam et

that the world was not favorable, " For this life is filled with innumerable labors and dangers by which the mind of a sage, although not entirely broken, nevertheless cannot be undisturbed, unless he should be altogether lacking in feeling." [45] Fazio too felt that, considering the state of the world, an internal solution was necessary for man, but he thought that the repression of the desires was insufficient, since it also meant a miserable struggle for man. Religion, wisdom, faith, hope and charity were also necessary. [46] " Yet by this alone can we be blessed in this life: if we seem least blessed to ourselves, if fleeing the allurements of pleasures and serving virtue alone, we live in all the miseries and labors which are the exercises and strengthenings of virtue, if finally we keep to that rough and difficult road which is opened up for us towards blessedness." [47] Man must strive to be the virtuous sage and man of letters that the humanists thought themselves to be, but he must not think that he will be any more secure or happy as one, " For you see many men of outstanding talent and learning are suffering for lack of personal income, lying prostrate, neglected by the wealthy, spurned by princes, of whom there is hardly anyone in this time of ours who favors the talents of men of letters." [48]

elegantiam quae ad victum cultumque corporis necessariae atque honestae sint, presentique rerum statu contentum esse, nec sentire se ulla re indigere, nihil expetere, nulli quaestui servire, omni denique animi anxietate, omni corporis carere molestia."

45 *Ibid.*, p. 30, " Est enim innumerabilibus laboribus et periculis referta haec vita: quibus etsi non omnino frangi, tamen non commoveri sapientis animus non potest, nisi penitus sensu caruerit."

46 *Ibid.*, p. 133.

47 *Ibid.*, pp. 133-34, " Hoc uno tamen beati esse in hoc vita possumus, si nobis beati esse minime videamur, si fugientes illecrebras voluptatum, solique virtuti servientes in omnibus miseriis, laboribusque vivamus quae sunt exercitia et corroboramenta virtutis, si denique illam asperam viam difficilemque teneamus, quae nobis ad beatitudinem patefacta est."

48 *Ibid.*, p. 86, " Vides enim multos viros, ingenio ac doctrina praestanti, rei familiaris inopia laborare, iacere humi, negligi a locupletibus, a principibus contemni, quorum fere nullus est, hac nostra tempestate, qui literatorum ingeniis faveat..." Cited by Thorndike, *op. cit.*, p. 187, n. 23.

Because Fazio was equally pessimistic about life in this world when the senses were given free rein and when they were held in check, his conception of man's nature emphasized the divine and spiritual attributes which, he believed, would make it possible for man to escape his weaknesses and miseries in the next life. The division and conflict between reason and passion was not conceived so sharply as by the former group of humanists. In fact Fazio tended to recognize that reason is one of the gifts of partial divinity in man which enable him even in this life to engage in many worldly activities, which, in spite of the misery they inevitably involve, contribute to the gratification of the senses. This recognition of the possible harmony of reason and sensual desire in a direct attack on nature led him to write in an optimistic mood about the power of the human mind over the world in a fashion similar to St. Augustine [49] and Manetti.[50] Thus " men have known secrets, constructed cities, invented shelter and clothing, founded laws, apprehended the turnings of the heavens and the motions and course of the stars, discovered medicine, besides so many arts, so many sciences such as among the first, philosophy, that master and leader of good living which first incites and establishes in us the worship of God and thence all works of virtue." [51] But since all earthly pursuits and occupations bring misery to man,[52] to what avail are these powers of the mind except to employ them in contemplation of divine things?

49 See above, pp. 28-29.

50 See above, pp. 71-72.

51 *De excellentia* etc. *op. cit.,* p. 152, "homines occulta cognoverint, urbes aedificaverint, tecta et vestimenta adinvenerint, leges condiderint, coelorum conversiones ac siderum motus cursusque deprehenderint, medicinam, tot praeterea artes, tot scientias, excogitaverint, ut inprimis philosophiam, illam bene vivendi magistram ac ducem, quae nos primum ad Dei cultum deinde ad omnia virtutis opera cohortatur atque institutit."

52 See the closing exhortation, *Ibid.,* pp. 167-68 and *De viri felicitate,* the entire first book leads to the conclusion, p. 92, ". . . nec in divitiis, nec in potentia, nec in amplitudine dignitatis, nec in regno, nec in gloria, nec in re militari, nec in agrorum cultura, nec in sacerdotio, nec in studiis literarum hanc esse quam quaerimus felicitatem. . ."

Francesco Filelfo's theory of human nature also divided the soul into reason and passions.[53] He accepted Plato's opinion that the soul had a rational part known as the mind and an irrational part governed by the two passions of anger and cupidity.[54] When the rational part suppresses the passions, the threefold virtue of intelligence, reason and morality can flourish. Man can achieve complete happiness, however, only by gaining the supreme good which "is nothing but God." But virtue is a mediary good which teaches the road by which happiness can be gained.[55] Men can live according to wisdom, virtue or pleasure. Those of greatest genius prefer the contemplative life. Those who are apt in practical affairs are delighted by the civil way of living and prefer virtue. But others, who he sees are very many, give themselves entirely to pleasure, and to that kind of pleasure which men have in common with cattle. They violate their human nature, which demands something better, and as a result are, of course, miserable. Men are distinguished from animals in their pleasures by the fact that animals are led merely by sense and impulse, while men follow reason and intellect. "For insofar as pleasure is concerned; can any greater or more permanent pleasure be gained than such as is gotten from virtuous actions or speculation on celestial or divine things?"[56] Indeed, Filelfo can't help being amazed at men "who, forgetful of themselves and of God, pursue nothing with greater zeal than either the deceitful blandishments of fortune or the softest allurements of the body, seeing that all those things are weak and perishable and little lasting."[57]

53 *De Morali Disciplina Libri Quinque,* Venice, 1552, written when he was 77, as he states pp. 54-5, therefore about 1475.

54 *Ibid.,* pp. 3-6.   55 *Ibid.,* p. 19.

56 *Ibid.,* p. 37, "Nam quod ad voluptas attinet; quae maior ulla, quae permanentior voluptas afferi queat; quam illa que vel ex honestis actionibus, vel ex rerum coelestium atque divinarum speculatione percipitur?"

57 *Ibid.,* p. 38, ". . . qui sui Deique obliti, nihil maiore sequuntur studio quam vel subdolas fortunae blanditias vel mollissimas corporis illecebras, quandoquidem ista omnia et infirma sunt et caduca parumque duratura."

Probably Filelfo's own life corresponded as little with the ideals he set forth as the most inconsistent of the humanists, for his reputation as a devotee of pleasure and as a cringing flatterer or a literary blackmailer when a more handsome reward might be wrung from a patron is well known.[58] Yet what he has to say about how little true satisfaction pleasure and material reward bring one, coming as it does at the end of a long life full of experience in pursuing pleasure and gain, need not imply that Filelfo was entirely hypocritical. No one could know better than he what difficulties might be involved in gaining prosperity and furthering a reputation. Yet he was in a position to see how much of an incentive material rewards were, and how general was this human failing. At the time that he wrote virtuous arts and studies were languishing because so many put material prosperity first. He thought that many writers were apt to neglect their studies if they found that their talents went unrewarded.[59] This could happen only because it was so common to take up the study of letters for profit rather than immortal glory. As for himself, of course, " there was never room with me for even the slightest suspicion of avarice." [60] And he should have known, for he had been well rewarded in his time. Indeed to no one were handsomer rewards given than to Francesco Filelfo alone, who was given so many thousands of gold coins that if he had preferred collecting treasure to following the call of learning and praise, he would have lacked nothing at the present time for every cultivation and elegance of life.[61] Bad times have fol-

58 See e.g. J. A. Symonds, *The Revival of Learning,* 2nd ed. London, 1898, pp. 204-06; and s.v. " Filelfo," *Encyclopedia Britannica,* 11th ed.

59 *Op. cit.,* p. 54, " Nam quotumquemque reperias, qui animadvertens fore, ut studia sua, quamvis pulcherrima sint, nullo habeantur in pretio, non ingenio veluti langueat, reddaturque aliorum negligentia tardisculus? "

60 *Idem.,* ". . . nulli unquam ne minimae quidem avaritiae suspicioni aut fortunae cuiuspiam vel blanditiis vel minis fuisse apud me locum . . ." This is, of course, hypocrisy, but Filelfo could still be sincere in worrying about the best way for a humanist to achieve happiness.

61 *Idem.*

lowed those great days, and men of learning are now neglected. That fact spurred him to write this treatise. He is worried not so much about his own hardships, since he is seventy-seven and too old to have to suffer much longer, as he is afraid that learning will decline with the neglect of men of learning.[62] That is the reason for his counsel " that all human happiness and blessedness is found in honesty alone and intelligence of mind." [63] Anyone who thinks he can find it otherwise is most miserable. The present frugality of cities and rulers should not be counted a hardship, then. When the Spartans were poor and virtuous they were great and free; and the same was true of the Romans, " who when they first had desired riches went completely to ruin." [64] Inner composure is only possible when virtue rather than gain is sought, for then " the soul is disposed to virtuous and distinguished actions through quiet, tranquil and composed affections suiting all parts."[65]

Filelfo's idea, that man can place himself on the road to composure through restraining his passions, was by his own admission evolved out of his personal experience and his observation of others. The desire for well-being and prosperity was being frustrated by the niggardliness of the great men upon whom writers depended for support. There was clearly no hope from that source. At the same time he knew that he had in the past been well rewarded, but still he felt that the way of worldliness was not the one for man. In other words, his own material success had shown him the illusory character of success. Contentment had to be found by the opposite method.

His conception of man, then, in spite of his violation of his own theories of conduct, required here also a withdrawal from

62 *Ibid.,* pp. 54-5.

63 *Ibid.,* p. 55, ". . . in sola probitate ac mentis intelligentia positam esse et constitutam humanam omnem felicitatem ac beatitudinem."

64 *Idem.,* "qui ubi primum divitiis studuissent, radicitus corruerunt."

65 *Idem.,* " disponi animum ad honestas praeclarasque actiones, per sedatas, ac tranquillas easdemque compositas, et in omnes partes convenientes affectiones."

a direct relationship with the world and a reliance on introversion, on internal suppression of desires. He was like the
Stoicizing humanists in the effect of what he was saying, but
in his additional requirement of contemplation of the divine
and eventual union with the divine he came closer in the actual
statement of his ideas to Fazio and to the Neoplatonic
humanists, Giovanni Pico and Marsilio Ficino.

Giovanni Pico della Mirandola's conception of human nature was shown clearly enough in his treatise on the *Dignity
of Man* that was discussed in the previous chapter.[66] It will
be remembered that he conceived of man as at his best when
he had risen above both vegetable torpor and bestial passion
to live according to reason and, still better, intelligence. If
he lived on the fourth and highest level, he approached the
divine. While he did not here conceive of an inner struggle
taking place between the parts of the human soul, nevertheless his idea of the four-fold choice of natures according to
which man might live, together with his favoring of the
third and fourth choices, placed him definitely with those who
rejected a worldly life. Dignity and superiority, equal to security and prestige ordinarily sought directly from worldly society,
could be gained only by rising above worldly society, for to
seek its rewards directly meant, for Pico, to live bestially according to the passions. He was less resigned about man's
potentialities than the humanists just studied, however, for
the higher level of life was for him open to all and attainable
by all, whereas others held that a struggle was necessary and
that the achievement was a rarity. Even Fazio, whose ideas
ran closest to Pico's, stated, in closing his treatise on the
Excellence of Man, that as in warfare only those soldiers who
fight most bravely and undertake the most difficult and severe
tasks are rewarded, so in human life, "not all who cultivate
the Christian faith but only those who, armed against these
human gifts and allurements, show themselves unconquered

66 See above, pp. 66-67.

and innocent of these must be held worthy of this so eminent and so divine reward of dignity." [67]

Marsilio Ficino, the best known Neoplatonist of the humanists, had a conception of man that followed closely after St. Augustine's view that man was miserable whether prosperous in the goods of this world or strictly virtuous. In a brief and succinct *Argument on the Supreme Good* [68] and again in a letter on *Happiness* [69] to Lorenzo de' Medici summing up a discussion between the two he presented his point of view. Human happiness is not to be found in goods of fortune such as money, power and honors, since they are sought for the body or the soul and bring cares, dangers, and enemies.[70] Nor is it to be found in bodily good, which is subject to the slightest injury and easily lost.[71] It has to be found, again by an internal adjustment, in the goods of the soul. But it is not found through the irrational part of the soul which possesses the power of acuteness and enjoys pleasures, since many animals excel man in acuteness, and since pleasures are often mixed and followed by many, long, heavy sorrows.[72] It is not found in the exercise of the natural powers of the rational part of the soul such as acumen, memory, boldness of will, because they can be employed for evil purposes.[73] It has to consist therefore in the acquired powers or virtues. But not in the moral virtues, as the group of humanists first discussed

67 *Op. cit.*, p. 168, ". . . non omnes qui Christianam fidem colunt, sed ii tantum qui contra hasce humanas opes atque illecrebras armati sese ab his invictos castosque praebent, hoc tam eximio ac tam divino dignitatis praemio digni habendi sunt."

68 *Argumentum de Summo Bono*, in Paulus Oscarius Kristeller, *Supplementum Ficinianum*, Florence, 1937, vol. II, pp. 96-7.

69 " Quid est felicitas, quod habet gradus, quod est aeterna," *Opera Omnia*, 2nd ed. of Henricpetri, Basel, 1576, pp. 662-65.

70 *Opera*, p. 662 and *Argumentum op. cit.*, p. 96. The letter and *Argument* follow each other very closely, the former being more elaborate.

71 *Opera*, p. 662.

72 *Idem.*

73 *Idem.*

thought; the struggle to suppress the passions involved in moral virtues brings suffering and anxiety along with it. It can be achieved only through the speculative virtues—contemplation of God.[74] It can only be gained after this life when the soul has been separated from the body, since the soul is continually subject to doubts and worries while in the body.[75]

Ficino, too, conceived of human nature as divided into conflicting parts at war with each other: the soul is at war with the body; the rational soul with the irrational, passionate soul; the rational soul divided into natural powers, neutral so far as the conflict is concerned, and acquired powers; its acquired powers divided into moral and speculative virtues, the moral virtues bearing the brunt of the conflict with the passions, the speculative virtues bringing the absolute peace and quiet of beatitude [76] only when finally the soul has been separated from the body in the act of enjoying the vision of God.[77]

Ficino's theory both in the manner in which it is set forth didactically and in its content seems reminiscent of the scholastic argument of Saint Thomas Aquinas on happiness.[78] Nevertheless, as would be expected in a writer so strongly committed to Neoplatonism, there are important differences. Thomas had emphasized that happiness coming in the beatific vision was an intellectual matter consisting of the knowledge of God; the pleasure of the will was merely an effect of this supreme end. Ficino, however, was true to the Augustinian tendency to emotionalize. He argued that since enjoyment is better than knowledge, love of God is better than knowledge of God in this life. That is so because no one truly knows God; as it is worse to hate God than to be ignorant of Him, so it is better to love than to know Him; knowledge of God may be badly

74 *Idem.*

75 *Opera,* p. 663.

76 *Opera,* p. 665.

77 *Opera,* p. 664.

78 See above, pp. 33-36.

used and lead to arrogance (does this fit Thomas' attitude?), whereas love can only be well used since it is self-denying. The knowledge of God adds nothing to God while love does add to God. One may know God for a long time with little profit but cannot help gaining a great profit from loving God even a short time. We receive more pleasure from loving and are better affected. Perhaps recognizing the need for a human motivation of otherworldliness, Ficino points out that we seek to see God for joy and not to enjoy God in order to see Him.[79] He continues that by knowing God we reduce Him to the capacity of our intellect and by loving we increase our will to His dimensions.[80]

Corresponding to Ficino's reliance on an otherworldly solution of man's quest for security was his pessimism over this life. Early in his career, he had written a long treatise on *Pleasure*.[81] This work by no means shows him to have been favorable toward worldliness, for it consists of a digest of the views of Plato, Aristotle, the Stoics and the Epicureans on the subject. He specifically declared both in his proem and his conclusion that he was not stating his own views but giving the opinions of philosophers.[82] His own attitude about this world can be found in the series of letters to close friends which in 1478 he ordered assembled and had translated into Italian as *Moral Sermons on the Stupidity and Misery of Men* [83] for

79 *Opera, sup. cit.*, p. 663.

80 *Opera*, p. 664.

81 *De Voluptate ad Anthonium Canisianum, Opera*, vol. I, pp. 986-1012.

82 *Ibid.*, pp. 986, 1012.

83 *Sermoni morali della stultitia et miseria degli uomini*, Codex Riccardianus 2684, membr., s. XV and Codex Magliabecchianus, VI, 238, cart., misc., s. XV, ff. 215-27v. See Kristeller, *op. cit.*, vol. I, p. xx. Kristeller prints *Prohemium*, II, p. 72, and collates the sermons, I, xx, with Latin letters "suis familiaribus" as printed in *Opera, op. cit.* They are as follows:

I	MS. Ric., f.	2	Op. p.	751	letter	beginning	Nemo est...
II	" " "	4	" "	749	"	"	Nullum in...
III	" " "	8	" "	784	"	"	Animus mortalibus... and p. 774 Quod animus...
IV	" " "	11	" "	637	"	"	Stultitia et ... (Vannio)

Jacopo di Guiccardini. In them he stated that " those who are more inclined to give themselves up to pleasures more frequently fall into sorrows." [84] Men not only suffer many evils in the present life but actually increase them by having no thought for the future,[85] " since the natural condition of this region so arranges that we may make use of sense, as if beasts, far earlier than reason, as if men." [86] There are many ways of being bestial but only one of being human. For we are divine in mortal wrappings and must separate the soul from the body and reason from the affections of the senses.[87] But still the great majority " so choose that fortune may follow their desires; that moreover desire may not follow reason, they care nothing." [88]

Matteo Bosso belongs with those who felt that security from hardship was not to be gained either by making a direct onslaught upon the world or by the cultivation of virtue and piety, since the former course brought brief pleasure and prestige mixed with powerfully disturbing passions and the latter course meant definite physical deprivation. After he became director of the Canonicate of St. Bartholomew at Fiesole and confessor to Lorenzo de' Medici, Bosso, through his interest in literature, oratory and philosophy, came into close

Footnote continued

V	MS. Ric., f.	13	Op.	p.	636	letter beginning Stultitia et ...		
VI	"	"	" 14v	"	" 637	"	"	Stultitia et ... (Landino)
VII	"	"	" 16v	"	" 640	"	"	De stultitia ...
VIII	"	"	" 17v	"	" 640	"	"	Cum bene omnia ...
IX	"	"	" 18v	"	" 659	"	"	Cognitio et ...
X	"	"	" 21	"	" 783	"	"	Leges divinae ...
XI	"	"	" 22v	"	" 652	"	"	De legi ...

Citations according to Latin letters.

84 *Opera,* p. 784, ". . . qui voluptatibus propensius obsequuntur ii saepius incidunt in dolores."

85 *Ibid.,* p. 752.

86 *Ibid.,* p. 775, " quia naturalis regionis huius conditio sic institutit ut longe prius sensu tanquam bruta quam ratione tanquam homines uteremur."

87 *Ibid.,* p. 659.

88 *Ibid.,* p. 637, " Optant ut cupiditates eorum fortuna sequatur, ne autem cupiditas rationem sequatur, nihil curant."

association with the Neoplatonists at Florence, especially Giovanni Pico.[89] Like others of this group, Bosso, in his dialogue on *Adversities to be Borne*[90] also looked to the next world for a release from suffering for the virtuous and for absolute misery for the worldly. To a complete pessimism about this life, he added, therefore, a final optimism about the next, making it clear that the hard road of virtue in this world was the one to choose.

The stated motive for writing this work was to console those who were suffering hardships.[91] Bosso attempts in it to answer the worldly arguments of a friend who looks upon man's place in the world perversely. The friend is shocked to find that those who give free rein to their passions and seek to make a good place for themselves in this world seem to prosper, while it is only the good and virtuous who suffer poverty, low position, exile, diseases and other calamities. Thus it seems of greater advantage to follow the world, as "all pale at the threshold of virtue and think it more advantageous to pass along the flat and blooming road than the steep and rough one, so that more service is paid to honors, dignities, desires and lusts than to God and the virtues."[92]

Bosso's reply is first that worldly delights are illusory. Because man is partially divine in nature, his final end is the heavenly life. Yet for a time he has to live on earth. Earthly pleasures are therefore more tangible and concrete, while the future true place of man seems abstract and distant, so that in this life man is the victim of an illusion that pleasure of

89 Girolamo Tiraboschi, *Storia della letteratura italiana*, Rome, 1783, vol. VI, part i, pp. 376-7.

90 *De Tolerandis adversis dialogus*, in *Recuperationes Fesulanae*, Florence, 1492?.

91 *Ibid.*, f. A3a.

92 *Ibid.*, f. A4b, " Pavescunt omnes in limine et perambulare plana atque virentia quam abrupta et salebrosa satius putant, ita honoribus, ita dignitatibus, ita cupiditatibus, ita libidinibus magis quam deo atque virtutibus inservitur."

the senses is genuine and restraint of desires truly painful.[93] Actually, however, " riches foster lust and procreate licentious-ness. Power, dignities, honors and the other things of this sort, which are valued according to what we have called false opinion, give birth to arrogance, nourish ambition, feed rage, reach toward hatred, envy, betrayals, parricides and poison-ings." [94] Even beauty of the body encourages prostitution and gluttony, and love for wife or children easily leads to crime.[95]

Secondly, there are numerous reasons, if the situation were truly seen, why it is ultimately better to choose the hardships, deprivations and inner struggles of a virtuous life. By sup-pressing his desires and living a hard life of virtue, man is able to avoid the corruption of the soul incumbent upon seek-ing security and ease in this world. Rome suffered corruption and decayed only after it had acquired an empire. The philo-sophers, Plato, Socrates and others, the saints and martyrs of the Church, all considered it better to suffer than to be corrupted.[96] The hardships of virtue also drive man to over-come torpor, inertia, and indifference, making it possible ulti-mately to see the truth. In the present time Alexander Gonzaga, the hunchback, was thus driven by his affliction to live a pious life devoted to learning, and Malatesta Novella, after becom-ing an incurable invalid, turned to philosophy, collected learned men about him, and built the greatest library in Italy.[97] It is a good thing that virtue entails suffering for the further reason that such suffering helps to atone for the evil inherent in human generation. Suffering is, therefore, not itself evil but the result of evil. This does not contradict man's possession of free will.

93 *Ibid.*, ff. A5a-b.

94 *Ibid.*, f. A5b, " Divitiae libidinem fovent et lasciviam procreant. Potentia dignitates honores et huiusmodi reliqua quae opinione falsi qua diximus in pretio sunt superbiam pariunt, ambitionem enutriunt, iram aluunt, odium, invidentiam, proditiones, parricidia, venenaque intentant."

95 *Idem.*

96 *Ibid.*, ff. A6a-A8a.

97 *Ibid.*, ff. A8b-B2a.

Freedom does not apply to the natural inconstancy, fragility, and uncertainty which come from man's inferior state in this world. It is this inferiority rather than lack of freedom that makes him so subject to evil. The allegation that he is without freedom is false, since, of course, man does have freedom over certain areas of his conduct.[98] It is not an injustice for the virtuous to suffer, because the example of the martyrs teaches that those who especially suffer are especially rewarded.[99] The virtuous should also suffer to prove their faith to themselves and to be an example to others.[100] The real and final reason why it is better to be virtuous and suffer hardships is the possibility of gaining the promised reward of heavenly life and the certainty of eternal punishment, if the hard road is not chosen for the brief period of this life.[101]

Bosso's theories were such as would put him definitely among those who thought that human nature was so formed that neither pursuit of material gain nor a life of virtue brought man much besides misery in this world and who believed that only in the other world man could lead a happy life above the limitations of the senses and the reason. Yet an interesting nuance in his thought placed him almost in the position of affirming the superiority of the passions for securing human comfort in this world. The Stoicizing humanists, as has been seen, denied the possibility of any satisfaction coming from the senses but felt that through suppressing the passions by reason, some few men might find existence tolerable in this world. The humanists, who are now being examined, denied the value for man both of a sensual and a reasonable life. Bosso did the same. He gave the impression, however, in the strong case for materialism which he had his antagonist state in the dialogue, in his own rather hasty slurring over the miseries of worldliness, and in his continual, heavy

98 *Ibid.*, ff. B2a-B4a.
99 *Ibid.*, ff. B4b-B5b.
100 *Ibid.*, ff. B5b-B6b.
101 *Ibid.*, ff. B6b-B8a.

emphasis upon the hardships of virtuous and pious life,—that perhaps, after all, so far as this life is concerned, self-seeking has its rewards. If the assurance of a future existence in the world beyond could be destroyed, there would be little incentive and less reason for putting down the persistent yearnings for comfort, security and prestige. But this was no more than a slight emphasis in Bosso, perhaps no greater than that of others who had taken a similar view and who felt that it was not comfort, security and prestige that were bad, but the brevity of them and the difficulty of getting them. Bosso's attitude was not ascetic so much as it was otherworldly, and in this respect he was extremely close to St. Augustine.[102]

The two groups so far examined regarded human nature as unfavorable for personal happiness. Their ideas ranged from (1) condemnation of sensual gratification and exaltation of rational suppression of desires through (2) condemnation of both passion and reason, to (3) partial recognition of pleasure and material values as pleasing to man, if attainable. The last came out of a realistic recognition of the hardships involved in the suppression of the passions through reason which was necessary for a future happiness. The first group held generally to the first view but tended in some cases to hold the second theory as well. The second group held generally the second opinion but sometimes approached the third attitude in emphasis. Both groups, in varying degree, conceived of a conflict between the ends of the feelings and of reason which made for inner human suffering.

In varying degree also (as the next chapter will study in greater detail), they conceived of the exterior world as inadequate or as elusive of man's grasp. Their ideas about human life were pessimistic both in regard to the make-up of man and in regard to man's functioning within the kind of environment the world provided. Man could be happy for all of them, except some of the Stoicizing group, only when the conflict

102 See above, p. 25.

of passion and reason came to an end and the environment of this world had been exchanged for a more favorable future world. For the exceptions, similar conditions for happiness were necessary—the complete blotting out of the emotions by reason, thus ending the conflict by conquest rather than mediation, and the achievement, through this conquest, of indifference to the environment, thus eliminating the world. None could bring himself to make his picture of man in the world an enthusiastic one.

Not all humanists viewed man so gloomily, and it would leave a decidedly misleading impression if some attention were not devoted to the viewpoints which were favorable to human nature. Some felt that the division of the human soul into the senses and the reason was not a sad condition, because there did not need to be a conflict between the demands of the two parts. The senses could have their satisfactions and the reason its virtues in harmony and contentment. Man, however, could not be happy just on this account, if his surroundings did not make it possible for pleasures to be enjoyed and virtues to be practiced. For this harmonious view of man, a favorable estimation of the outside world was also required, if man was to be considered truly content with this life.

Two well known humanists of the first half of the fifteenth century, Leonardo Bruni and Lorenzo Valla, held such favorable views of man. The former was known as an Aristotelian and the latter as an Epicurean. Bruni expressed his attitude simply, clearly and unpretentiously in a brief *Isagogicon of Moral Discipline,* written, according to Baron, after his translation of the *Nichomachean Ethics,* probably about 1421-1424.[103] After arguing the superiority of moral philosophy to science as it is more useful to man, Bruni explained that all

---

103 *Isagogicon moralis disciplinae,* pp. 20-41, Hans Baron, *Leonardo Bruni Aretinos Humanistische-Philosophische Schriften,* Leipzig, 1928. Walter L. Bullock in a review of Baron's edition, *Speculum IV* (1929), pp. 476-83, states, p. 483, that it is " sadly unreliable for the study of Bruni's exact text, but a welcome and valuable contribution, actually indispensable, for the study of Bruni's ideas."

human desires and actions are subordinate to each other and to some ultimate end, that the end is the supreme good, and that man attains happiness by attaining the supreme good.[104] According to some, the Epicureans, everything is done for the sake of pleasure. Bodily pleasure is emphasized in varying degree by this group.[105] Others, the Peripatetics, feel happiness lies in the practice of virtue which means not merely to exist as plants, or feel as animals, but to carry on life according to reason.[106] This was Bruni's attitude also, and it differed from the Stoics' severity, "For they deny that anything is good except virtue . . . moreover, they deny that comforts of the body and of fortune are good, and contrarily they deny that their discomforts are evil." [107] Indeed, the welfare of the body and wealth is necessary both for happiness and to make the practice of virtue possible. Virtue alone does not suffice, " for it can happen that a wise and good man, educated in and adorned by all the virtues, may be forced into exile, bereavement and poverty, losing fatherland, his fortune taken away, children and relatives murdered; besides he may fall into the prison of a tyrant, the rack, severe and miserable punishment. Who therefore can say that he, although abounding in virtues, is nevertheless blessed among such great evils? . . . Moreover, they say it is necessary for man to have bodily and external goods, not that these in themselves make up a blessed life, but that the deeds of virtue, of which a blessed life consists, may not be hindered." The virtuous man is never miserable, but without security and well-being he is not happy.[108]

104 *Ibid.*, pp. 20-4.

105 *Ibid.*, p. 25.

106 *Idem.*

107 *Ibid.*, p. 26, " Negant enim quicquam (quicquid?) esse bonum praeter honestum, . . . Corporis autem et fortunae commoda negant esse bona, contraque illorum incommoda negant mala esse."

108 *Ibid.*, pp. 25-6, " Fieri enim potest, ut sapiens et bonus vir et omnibus virtutibus instructus atque ornatus in exsilium, in orbitatem, in egestatem detrudatur, amissa patria, ablato patrimonio, filiis propinquisque necatis; praeterea, ut in carcerem tyranni, ut in equuleum, ut in supplicia gravia et

So far, Bruni's theories seem to come close to those who felt that both absence of physical and social well-being and virtuous control of the feelings by reason made happiness impossible. Where Bruni differed was in his confidence that man is so composed that a harmonious adjustment between the irrational sensible part of the soul and the rational part was possible. Virtue for him is not the suppression of the desires but their moderation into a habit of behavior and affection between the two extremes of feeling. This was moral virtue.[109] Moderation was achieved by the intellectual virtue of prudence—right reason directing the passions into the moderation of moral virtue.[110] Thus man could achieve fortitude as the mean between foolhardy boldness and cowardice, or liberality as the mean between prodigality and avarice.[111]

Such a view of the harmonious internal adjustment of man, however, was not held absolutely by Bruni, for he too conceived of man as being dual, and the conciliation of the two parts of the soul, while possible, was not always easy. Prudence had to assert its directive powers, and sometimes it would succeed in achieving virtue and sometimes it would fail, " for it is difficult to curb the passions as if by a bridle, difficult to hold back anger, difficult to coerce avarice." [112] In some cases it was impossible, for unless a man is naturally good, he lacks the intellectual virtue of prudence altogether.[113]

The real mark of Bruni's breadth of view was the absence of the idea that man either lived according to his passions or according to his reason. For Bruni, closely following Aristotle,

---

miseranda incidat. Hunc igitur, quamquam virtutibus adunantem, tamen beatum dicere tantis in malis quis potest? . . . Corporis autem et externa adesse homini oportere aiunt, non ut illa ex sese beatam conficiant vitam, sed ne operationes virtutis, in quibus beata vita consistit, impediantur."

109 *Ibid.*, p. 29.

110 *Ibid.*, p. 38.

111 *Ibid.*, pp. 30-2.

112 *Ibid.*, p. 29, " Difficile est enim libidines quasi freno compescere, difficile iracundiam tenere, difficile avaritiam coercere."

113 *Ibid.*, p. 40.

although difficult, it was possible to gratify the feelings in moderation and at the same time to be rational. The first element of a thorough acceptance of human values was present in his thought, the approach toward a conception of human nature as an integrated whole rather than as at conflict with itself. But in so far as he conceived of personality as divided, his conception was open to denial of some aspects of life. The second element necessary for complete optimism was a favorable view of the external environment. Bruni gave no indication of what he thought of the world and his times in this treatise. He may therefore have been favorable to man but fearful about the world or his times. Bruni's reputation as a successful, self-made man, emphasized even by his contemporaries,[114] however, might suggest that so far as his own experience went, he could accept with some warmth the world and his times as well.

Another treatise that sets forth a high estimate of human powers is Lorenzo Valla's *Pleasure and True Good*.[115] This treatise presents some difficulty in interpretation, since it apparently was rewritten more than once by Valla, and it is hard to know which version represents his genuine views. The question arises whether Valla in the extant published versions toned down the force of his statements in favor of a voluptuary life. The fact that a different place and a different set of interlocutors were used in the Louvain and Basel editions has added to the confusion. According to Girolamo Mancini, however, the two printed versions have only " insignificant differences, limited to words and brief phrases " as far as the text is concerned.[116] As for Valla's intentions, Mancini be-

114 Baron, *Speculum*, XIII, p. 20, cites Poggio's condemnation of Bruni's thrift and ambition and Manetti's praise of the same in funeral orations.

115 *De Voluptate ac vero bono libri tres*, in *Opera Omnia*, Basel, 1540. The earlier editions were *Pangeticon de vero bono*, Louvain, 1483 and, as first cited, Basel, 1519. References will be to description by Max von Wolff, *Lorenzo Valla Sein Leben und Seine Werke*, Leipzig, 1893 and Girolamo Mancini, *Vita di Lorenzo Valla*, Florence, 1891.

116 Mancini, *op. cit.*, p. 46.

lieved that he meant to refute both extreme Epicureanism and Stoicism in order to achieve a position of Christian moderation.[117] Mancini also thought, that consistent with these ends, Valla actually strengthened the defense of voluptuarism he set up to refute when he prepared the final versions of his treatise. An incentive for doing this lay in Valla's quarrel with Panormità, who upheld pleasure in the treatise and whom Valla desired to blacken.[118]

Probably Valla had a number of previous treatises on the problem of happiness in mind. Mancini suggests that he was trying to reply to Zabarella's treatise on *Happiness*.[119] This work was also divided into three books showing that happiness was not in pleasure against the Epicureans, that temporal happiness lay in the practice of virtue, and the happiness of the blessed, respectively.[120] Mancini also believed that Valla was thinking of Mafeo Vegio and of the Stoic period of Bruni's ideas.[121]

That Valla had the *Isagogicon* of Bruni in mind when he wrote his own treatise on *Pleasure and True Good* is suggested by the first of the three books. It was devoted to expounding what Valla conceived the Stoic point of view to be, and Bruni was made its spokesman. Bruni in the *Isagogicon,* of course, considered himself an Aristotelian rather than a Stoic such as he had earlier been; nevertheless, Valla interpreted him somewhat inaccurately as believing that absolute virtue—*honestas*—was the *true* good, as opposed to Bruni's designation of it as the *supreme* good. On the other hand, Valla came close to understanding Bruni's definition of virtue as a mediate affection between the opposite extremes of the feelings. Thus there were twice as many sins as virtues, and

117 Mancini, *Ibid.,* pp. 61-2.

118 "Alcune Lettere di Lorenzo Valla," pp. 1-48, *Giornale storico della letteratura italiana,* XXI (1893), pp. 23-6.

119 *Op. cit.* Mancini, *Giornale storico,* etc., pp. 27-9.

120 Cf. Zonta, *op. cit.,* p. 20.

121 Mancini, *Vita* etc., chap. 3 and *Giornale storico* etc.

virtue consequently was so difficult to gain that most men
sought instead military fame, the pleasures of court life,
political power, or commercial or agricultural success.[122] Valla
in this way sharpened the conflict between a life of worldliness
and a life of virtue, which Bruni had viewed as being possibly
complementary. Yet Valla also misrepresented the Stoic point
of view, which he incorrectly attributed to Bruni, since he took
over the Aristotelian idea of Bruni that virtue was the result
of the moderation of the passions rather than their complete
suppression. Valla's version of Stoicism, while in this way
bridging over to some degree the cleft usually seen between
the reason and the emotions, still was extremely antagonistic
to the use of the emotional and sensual faculties. The innate
nature of man, because of the two-to-one odds against virtue,
was evil.[123] Furthermore, according to Valla's interpretation,
the Stoic regarded nature as the traditional enemy of man,
visiting him periodically with pestilence, famine, fire and other
calamities.[124]

In the second book Valla stated through Antonio Panormita
the view of extreme Epicureanism. If the Stoic was far-going
in seeing good only in virtue, Valla's Epicurean was even more
so in his emphasis on complete sensual gratification as
the only end of all human action, however concealed this end
might be behind high moral purposes. The Stoics' virtue was
in their own terms mythical since it was so difficult as to be
practically impossible to achieve and therefore amounted to
nothing.[125] Wealth, power, honor,[126] virtue and fame are
sought only as means to enjoyment; everything is measured
by the principle of personal utility. Men are kind and charit-
able to their fellows in expectation of enjoying some kindness
in return and to avoid making enemies who can cause them

122 Wolff, *op. cit.*, p. 17.
123 *Ibid.*, p. 18.
124 *Ibid.*, pp. 18-9.
125 *Ibid.*, pp. 19-20.
126 *Ibid.*, p. 21.

harm.[127] These are the true principles on which human nature is based, and everyone follows them in actual life, whatever theories he may hold. Stoic ideas have not prevented most men of the present age from leading an Epicurean life, enjoying fine meals and entertainments at each others homes.[128] The very limitations on enjoyment practiced in society have grown out of disguised egoistic motives. Thus feminine beauty brings the greatest of pleasure, and women should not hide their beautiful parts. The envy of old or deformed women was probably responsible for the unnecessary modesty that prevails.[129] The practices of virginity, celibacy, marital fidelity tend to deny full sensual pleasure and are pointless; the double standard allowing men more freedom than women has no basis, since women have as much right to lovers as men have. Monasticism must have been an invention of impotent and greedy old men.[130]

It seems probable that Valla subscribed neither to extreme Stoicism nor to extreme Epicureanism. He did not believe that virtue meant the complete denial and suppression of sensual desire, nor did he believe that pleasure of the senses was the only end of man, to which reason and pretensions of virtue were merely means. His own point of view was probably that expressed by Nicolò Niccoli, as the Christian, in the third book. This is the opinion of Max von Wolff [131] who felt that it was probable that Valla accepted the Christian rather than the Epicurean attitude. As has been seen, it is also the theory of Girolamo Mancini [132] who cited Fiorentino to the effect that Valla's reputation as a vulgar Epicurean, and an enemy of Christianity, was due to his own enemies, and that he was defending Christianity both from false, pagan materialism and

127 *Ibid.*, p. 29.
128 *Ibid.*, p. 30.
129 *Ibid.*, p. 22.
130 *Ibid.*, pp. 25-6.
131 *Ibid.*, pp. 14-5.
132 Mancini, *Vita*, etc., pp. 61-2.

from hypocritical, ascetic horror of pleasure.[133] At any rate
Valla, himself, in his proem, complains of the pagan tendencies
of his time and states that he wishes to show the true morality
of Christ by confronting it with the false pagan views.[134]
Moreover, in the statement of Christianity in the third book,
Niccoli attacks the onesidedness of both Stoicism and Epicureanism and affirms that both virtue and pleasure have their
place in human life, that one does not exclude the other, but
that reason and the senses can complement each other, although the danger of vice is always present.[135] Nature is
neither the implacable enemy of man nor simply to be enjoyed;
natural disasters are punishments for human sins. Both virtue
and earthly pleasure are secondary to a heavenly goal, and
man should love God before all. There is much pain and not
too much pleasure in this life, so it is best to be virtuous and
work for a heavenly reward.[136] The otherworldly note, re-
enforced by a detailed description of the glories, beauties and
delights of heavenly life,[137] contradicts somewhat the view
that pleasure and virtue are both possible and desirable on
earth, for Niccoli claims that without faith and hope in God,
virtue would be meaningless and pleasure the only goal of
man.[138] This seems to imply that in striving to be virtuous in
order to gain a future reward man must limit to some extent
his pursuit of earthly pleasure. Like Bruni, Valla was not
absolute in his view of the internal harmony of human nature,
for the danger of onesidedness was present, but, if the third
book does give his personal views, he definitely saw a proper
place for pleasure in this life and believed that an amicable
adjustment of the tendencies of the reason and the senses was

133 Vittorio Rossi, *Il Quattrocento*, Milan, 1897-8, p. 54, also holds that
Niccoli expresses Valla's views.

134 Wolff, *op. cit.*, p. 16.

135 *Ibid.*, pp. 31-2.

136 *Ibid.*, p. 33.

137 *Ibid.*, pp. 34-5.

138 *Ibid.*, p. 33.

possible even in preparation for a future life which the present foreshadowed.

Another example of a harmonious view of human nature is found in the discussion of *Happiness* by the late fifteenth century Bolognese humanist, Filippo Beroaldo.[139] Happiness consists for him of "abundance of desirable things."[140] It can be gained through no single end such as pleasure,[141] glory,[142] power,[143] wealth,[144] or virtue,[145] since each by itself has its own defects. It has to be gained through a combination of goods of the soul, the body and of fortune,[146] because "man is neither body alone, nor soul alone, but is composed from soul and body together."[147] Bodily goods are health, strength and beauty and are needed for the sake of the soul and to make possible the practice of virtues, the goods of the soul.[148]

Beroaldo's notions about man seemed to require a harmony of body and soul. Nevertheless, he laid certain limitations on the sufficiency of things necessary for bodily good because they caused inner disturbances of the soul. Pleasure often leads to evil and thus cancels or makes difficult the development of virtues, the goods of the soul.[149] Both power and wealth bring worry, fear, and other inner anguish.[150] He made it clear, however, that the inner turmoil sometimes accompanying the pursuit of external things was due not so much to a

139 *Oratio de foelicitate*, ff. 112-122, *Varia Opuscula Philippi Beroaldi*, Basel, 1513.

140 *Ibid.*, ff. 112a, 119b, "plenitudo rerum optandarum."

141 *Ibid.*, ff. 112b-114a.

142 *Ibid.*, ff. 114a-115b.

143 *Ibid.*, ff. 115a-116b.

144 *Ibid.*, ff. 116b-118b.

145 *Ibid.*, ff. 118b-120b.

146 *Ibid.*, ff. 121a-122b.

147 *Ibid.*, f. 119b, "Homo neque solum corpus est, neque anima sola, sed ex anima simul et corpore compactus est."

148 *Ibid.*, f. 120a.

149 *Ibid.*, f. 113b.

150 *Ibid.*, ff. 115b, 118a.

conflict in desires and aims of the parts of man as to the difficulty of attaining and maintaining the goods of fortune. His
affirmative view of the nature of man was not limited. Still
he was disheartened about human life, since the brevity and
uncertainty of worldly success [151] led him to conclude that " no
one is happy." [152] He recognized the possibility of bliss in a
future life, but his concern was primarily earthly happiness.[153]

To this group may be added Manetti, whose treatise on the
Dignity of Man [154] expressed a confidence that virtue and
pleasure can complement each other. Manetti's acceptance of
human values was also limited both by a recognition of the
competitive character of the human pursuit of dignity [155] and
by an otherworldliness which postponed to a future life the
compensations for the hardships and deprivations which virtue
sometimes involved.[156]

Baron emphasized Bruni and Manetti [157] in particular as
exponents of the need for the good things of this world to
make virtue a practicable affair. Other examples which he
gave were the fourth book of Matteo Palmieri (1405-1475)
on *Civil Life*,[158] the *Camaldulensian Disputations* of Cristoforo
Landino,[159] Giovanni Nesi on *Morals*,[160] the dedication of the

151 *Ibid.,* f. 115a, ". . . sit res caduca, et intra breve saeculum flaccescat
. . .", and f. 121a describing the arbitrary powers of fortune. See also below,
pp. 134-135.

152 *Ibid.,* f. 122a, " nemo est foelix."

153 *Ibid.,* f. 112b, " Ecclesiastici doctores summum bonum esse dixerunt
vitam aeternam . . . Sed nos in praesentia de humana felicitate disseramus."
He also chides the Stoics for their pride in asserting that a sage could
achieve happiness through virtue on earth, citing, f. 119b, St. Augustine,
De Civitate Dei, book xix.

154 See above, pp. 68-69.

155 See above, p. 70.

156 See above, pp. 73, 76

157 Baron, *Speculum,* XIII, pp. 20-2.

158 *Ibid.,* p. 23, *Della Vita Civile,* ed. Milan, 1830.

159 *Ibid.,* p. 25, *Disputationum Camaldulensium libri quatuor,* Venice, 1500.

160 *Ibid.,* p. 25, *De moribus,* described by Thorndike, *op. cit.,* pp. 187-91.

Misopenes of Pandolfo Collenuccio (1444-1504),[161] and the *Advantages of the Roman Curia* of Lapo da Castiglionchio, Jr. (1405?-1438).[162] There can be no doubt that there was a strong tendency among the humanists to reject the one-sided Neostoic view that man could get along without the objects of sensual desire and still remain contented in this world.

To Baron's list there might conceivably be added most of the group of humanists who urged the suppression of the sensual for otherworldly ends but who recognized that the attainment of virtue in this way meant a great deal of hardship and suffering for man. While they favored repression for the sake of virtue, they did not on principle hold a one-sided view of man. The pursuit of worldly goods seemed to them so involved with difficulties that, apart from the failure to gain prosperity, security or recognition which many men had to suffer, the very struggle, whether or not it ended in success, destroyed human composure and upset man internally. For this reason it was far better to choose the hard path of virtue, especially in view of the greater assurance of future bliss this entailed. And so, although this group also was aware of the physical and social needs of man, it was inclined to deny that man could be happy in this world, and although the group discussed last recognized that the hope of bliss in the world to come required the practice of virtue in this world, it saw a possibility of happiness here. The attitudes of the two groups were fundamentally different. Otherworldliness and belief in the inner antagonism of human nature were stronger in the one than in the other. Hence, along with the first Neostoic group, the second group must be considered negative toward human values, while the third group was positive in favoring them.

The views on human nature of the three groups, however, were quite similar and tended to melt into each other. It really comes down to shades of emphasis rather than sharp differ-

161 *Ibid.,* p. 28, *Misopenes,* in *Opera,* II, Bari, 1929.

162 *Ibid.,* p. 30, *De Curiae Romanae Commodis,* ed. R. Scholz, *Quellen und Forschungen aus italienischen Archiven,* XVI, 1914.

entiation of ideas. One of the deciding factors, as the next chapter will suggest, was the individual writer's estimate of the conditions of the world and society—whether the environment of man provided a favorable or adverse field in which to satisfy his desires. The sects or schools of philosophy— Stoic, Epicurean, Platonic, Aristotelian, or Eclectic—to which respect was paid, were not always interpreted purely but were usually fitted to the purposes of the writer, although the classical model probably came sympathetically close to the mood of the humanist. Ultimately, perhaps, it was experience which moulded the attitudes of a writer, as, for example, the frequent complaints about the niggardliness of patrons seem to show. Common to all, whether hostile or friendly, in their view of man, was a universal concern with the question of what was the best way to make the experience of human life satisfying and peaceful.

CHAPTER V
THE EXTERNAL CONDITIONS OF LIFE

It has been seen that some of the humanists so conceived of man's nature that a satisfactory internal adjustment was regarded either as extremely difficult or extremely rare and that others had a brighter view which held that internal harmony was quite possible. In both cases the attitude toward life in this world was conditioned by the attitude toward man's external environment as much as by the theories of the nature of man. It was suggested in this connection that recourse to an internal solution, whether easy or difficult, was symptomatic of a feeling of doubt whether the outside world could be readily moulded to meet desires for security, comfort or prestige. It may at first seem illogical that the humanists who considered internal harmony most rare or even impossible were most fearful about the external world as well, while those who felt that reason and the senses could easily be conciliated were happier about their surroundings.[1] If no peace were possible, no compromise acceptable between the desires of the feelings and the aims of reason, one or the other had to be given complete mastery. Either the feelings should seek full satisfaction in the goods of this world, or their desires should be exterminated by reason. If it was extremely difficult for satisfactory gratification to be achieved in the world, it would leave man indeed a miserable creature unless he heeded the dictates of reason. Recourse to suppression of desire by reason, hard as it was to achieve, was man's only possible way of escaping misery. Only the blackest view of the world could lead to this rigorous doctrine.

On the other hand, if, as in the happier views of man, some gratification of the emotions was possible, or even necessary, for the practice of virtue by the rational part of the soul, his

1 Excepting Beroaldo. His pessimism about the outer world, however, is a special case and arises out of the calamitous conditions of his period— about sixty years later than the others. See below, pp. 134-135.

attitude toward the outer world had simply to be one of trying to make the best of it. The human *modus vivendi* was in
this case not a sharp choice between extremes of passionate-
ness and rationality in which the latter was an imperative because of the objectively bad outer world. Life was rather a
taking of the world as it came, accepting its favors and re-
gretting its hardships but never fleeing from it, because the
only chance of making this life at all satisfying lay in facing
the world. Such an attitude, which Leonardo Bruni for example
carried out both in theory and practice, could come only out
of an initial acceptance, and not necessarily a blind or naive
acceptance, of the world, out of a confidence that one could
make one's way in life without too great difficulty. Appreciation of human qualities went along with appreciation of the
world, and doubt about the one accompanied doubt about the
other.

The feeling that the physical universe was hostile was rather
less frequent than a criticism of the inadequacy of society in
providing any permanent security, comfort, prestige or tranquillity for man whatever his pursuit. Of all the humanists who
were concerned about the end of man, Poggio Bracciolini in
The Misery of Human Condition gave the only clear-cut statement on the antagonism of nature to human life. Up until the
end of the fifteenth century and the early sixteenth century
social adjustment, the problem of finding a career that might
be truly satisfactory to the individual, seems to have been the
major worry. This tendency may correspond to their rootless-
ness as a group at first, to the fact that they were unattached
to any recognized institution. The problem of securing recognition of their cultural and even moral importance through the
identification of virtue with their literary activities was uppermost.[2] Later, when they were more firmly established and the

2 See above, Chapter III, especially the discussion of Salutati. That chapter covers much of the material, particularly on the question of the inadequacy of existing careers in society, the discussions of true nobility, etc.
and need not be repeated.

fashion of employing and patronizing humanists had spread, the problem of the present difficulties and of the future of society as a whole rather than of specific social positions, came to the fore. Discussion turned to the calamities of the time, what brought them on, how they might be avoided.

It has already been shown that the authors of works on *True Nobility* such as Buonaccorso, Poggio, Platina, as well as a man like Salutati looked down upon inherited position and upon high rank acquired through the accumulation of wealth.[3] Poggio continued the same line of thought in parts of his *Misery of Human Condition* [4] and even composed a separate treatise on the *Unhappiness of Rulers.*[5] Fazio spent the largest part of the first book of *Human Happiness* [6] in refuting claims that any profession or position of worldly distinction was sufficient for a happy life, and in the *Excellence of Man* he took pains to contrast the false gains coming from positions of worldly dignity with the genuine prestige of gaining spiritual excellence.[7] Petrarch, too, persuaded himself that much of his misery came from a futile pursuit of worldly honors.[8] Obviously all of these writers, and others as well, felt that something was wrong with society as they found it. Since so much of their criticism has already been discussed, it is needless to examine anything more than what specifically they felt was the trouble. Why did they feel that success according to the conventional social standards was more apt to bring misery than contentment?

There seem to be two reasons given for the undesirability of high position. First, the position itself is not what it seems; it usually carries certain burdens with it that increase with the loftiness of the position; it is very difficult to maintain and is

3 See above, Chapter III.
4 *Op. cit.,* pp. 99, 103.
5 *De infelicitate principum,* pp. 390-419, *Opera Omnia,* Basel, 1538.
6 *Op. cit.,* pp. 32-92.
7 *Op. cit.,* pp. 167-68, see above, pp. 68-69.
8 *Secretum, de contemptu mundi, op. cit.,* pp. 89-90, 72.

short-lived, as accident or fortune remove one from it; it is extremely difficult to gain in the face of a universal scramble for it. These are all external reasons. Secondly, both the struggle to gain the position and to retain it disturb the soul.[9] This seems, at first, to come out of the conception of human nature which held that the pursuit of sensual gratification ran counter to the objects of reason; that it was not the nature of society which was at fault but the nature of man. The first set of reasons, further, do not seem to be a criticism of society so much as a criticism of all social positions. Both sets of reasons, however, the inadequacy of the position, the effects of its pursuits on the soul, may be said to come from an implied criticism of the competitive nature of society. Sometimes it was clearly seen; Petrarch, for example, says, " All the world cannot possibly occupy the first and best place. How could there be a first unless there was also a second following after? Only be thankful, you mortal men, if you are not reduced to the last of all." [10] Manetti, in a passage already cited, also recognized it.[11] And Poggio stated that, " The people do not know how much envy can do in public affairs." [12] More often, it was not seen as a general condition of society, but as a tendency of human nature that had to be fought against.[13] It is clear, however, from the very concern of the humanists

9 Poggio, *De infelicitate principum, op. cit.,* pp. 416-17 for example claimed that the institution of rule was bad in its very nature because those men who were able to make themselves immune from the passions excited by ruling were overcome by the cares and responsibilities of office, or suffered the jealousy even of close friends or the tides of fortune; most men, however, were tormented by internal tortures because they were unable to escape anger, lust, avarice, ambition, fear, suspicion brought on by the struggle to keep their position.

10 *Op. cit.,* pp. 89-90.

11 See above, p. 70, *De dignitate et excellentia hominis, op. cit.,* pp. 161-62.

12 *De miseria humanae conditionis, op. cit.,* p. 103, " Ignorat populus quantum in Re Publica possit invidia...."

13 As for example, Fazio, *De excellentia ac praestantia hominis, op. cit.,* pp. 167-68.

with the problem of social position, that whether they saw it clearly or not, a competitive struggle for security and recognition lay behind their criticisms of high position, which often, as has been suggested before, helped to console them for their own failure. Petrarch was very precise on this, as a further citation from the passage just quoted will show. The competitive struggle is responsible for sorrows; the positions are really undesirable; forgetting them or rejecting them brings relief. " That which casts men down into these doleful moods is that each one, forgetting his own condition, dreams of the highest place, and, like everyone else, as I have just now pointed out, cannot possibly attain it; then when he fails he is discontented. If they only knew the sorrows that attend on greatness they would recoil from that which they pursue." [14]

Poggio and Manetti both were aware of the relation of man to the natural world, but in keeping with the rest of their attitudes, they looked upon nature from opposite points of view. To Manetti nature conferred many benefits and pleasures upon man, and it was the field of his activities in this world. It was praised as evidence of human greatness that God had placed so rich a storehouse of useful and beautiful things at man's disposal.[15] Among the bounties of nature he mentioned lands, fields, meadows, mountains, hills, valleys, the fig, plums, nuts, filberts, chestnuts, oaks, holm oaks, sycamores, fruits of all plants, domestic and wild animals, rivers, streams, birds, fish, the heavens, stars, planets, angels.[16] Poggio, on the other hand, devoted a long section of the *Misery of Human Condition* [17] to showing from his own experience that, " heaven, earth, water, air, fire, men, poverty, beasts, various disturbances of the soul bring the misery of life to us." [18] He saw floods cause

---

14 *Op. cit.,* p. 90.

15 *De dignitate et excellentia hominis, op. cit.,* p. 114, see above, p. 73.

16 *Ibid.,* pp. 134-35.

17 *Op. cit.,* pp. 108-11.

18 *Ibid.,* p. 110, " Coelum, terra, acqua, aer, ignis, homines, paupertas, belua, animorum variae perturbationes nobis vitae miseriam moliuntur."

great damage and loss of life at Marana, Burgo Campi, the Arno valley, Flanders. He witnessed terrible fires in Basel and Geneva.[19] Lack of air brings suffocation; bad air brings pestilence, disease and storms. Earth furnishes the metal for weapons and many poisons. Many men die from being struck with bolts of lightning, from the bites of spiders. Wild beasts threaten men, and even tame dogs bite and cows injure with their horns; horses kick. Excessive cold produces chills and fevers.[20] Poggio had no theory to explain the dangers of nature to man. He presented them as natural facts to be accepted as such. Life was therefore always and permanently miserable.

At the very close of the century Italy entered a disastrous period when the breakup of the alliance of Florence, Milan and Naples was followed by the French invasion in 1494. About the same time deaths from the new disease of syphilis, with which the physicians were at first unable to cope, began to occur. The series of invasions by foreign armies encouraged civil war in the Italian states and led to the frequent overturn of rulers and governments in which opposing parties played their role. There was an increase in the number of exiles and in the violence of political life.[21] The humanists were naturally involved in the political fortunes of their patrons and suffered. Some of them, as will be seen, came to look upon their own times as calamitous and wrote about " our calamities " and pondered their immediate and remote causes. No longer, as in the case of Poggio, did they regard political disasters or natural calamities—fire, flood, pestilence, famine which they associated with the wars, assassinations, seditions, proscriptions and exiles as part of the general condition of the times —as a permanent state of affairs or as a natural, inexplicable condition. The crying problem for them was the present state

19 *Ibid.*, pp. 108-09.

20 *Ibid.*, pp. 109-110.

21 This was, of course, not the first period of "calamities." The wave of pestilence concentrated around the Black Death in the fourteenth century, as well as the Hundred Years' War, had influenced writers.

of society and not their individual security and equanimity. There could be no peace and security for them until there was peace and security in society at large. Perhaps also there was no longer quite the same need to justify the humanist way of life.

In 1506 Giovanni Corsi wrote a *Life of Ficino*.[22] In it he emphasized the felicity of the humanists before the disasters of 1494. But from that time on it was not the niggardliness of rulers but social turmoil and the general calamity which affected the humanists. Referring to the exile of the Medici and the uprising of 1494 he emphasized that "the calamity of our times is especially to be mourned on this account, since in our city stupidity and ignorance rule instead of the disciplines and good arts, avarice instead of liberality, ambition and lust instead of modesty and continence, even so that nothing is done altogether for the commonwealth, nothing legally, but all for reason of lust in such a way that each leading citizen is assailed with derision by the mob. Detesting this as one would a most severe stepmother, Bernardo Oricellari recently went into voluntary exile rather than be longer in that city whence the disciplines of all good arts as well as the best customs of the elders went into exile together with the Medici."[23] Clearly it was necessary for the humanists to discover the roots of the calamities and propose the corresponding remedies, for their entire future was bound up with the fate of Italian society.

22 *Vita Ficini,* ed. Bandini, printed in Galetti, *Philippi Villani Liber de Civitatis Florentiae Famosis Civibus . . . et de Florentinorum Litteratura Principes fere Synchroni Scriptores,* Florence, 1847.

23 *Ibid.,* p. 189, "quocirca nostrorum temporum calamitas maxime miseranda quandoquidem in nostra civitate pro disciplinis ac bonis artibus, inscitia et ignorantia, pro liberalitate, avaritia, pro modestia et continentia, ambitio et luxuria dominantur; atque adeo ut nihil omnino cum Republica, nihil cum legibus agatur, sed pro libidine cuncta, ita ut optimus quisque a plebe per ludibrium oppugnetur. Quam veluti saevissimam novercam detestatus nuper Bernardus Oricellarius exsulandum sibi duxit potius quam diutius esse in ea urbe, unde una cum Medicibus omnium bonarum artium disciplinae atque optima majorum instituta exsularent."

A frequent explanation for the visitations of calamities was that they were a means of carrying out divine justice on earth. Marsilio Ficino himself, who had earlier called his age abounding in golden geniuses,[24] argued now that men were always allowed to suffer innumerable evils so that they would learn to distinguish good from evil, to purge the curable and punish the incurable sinners.[25] There was no remedy open to man. Only if God desired, He might warn men through the medium of some prophet to change their ways in time to avoid the impending disasters.[26] The Florentines had thus been saved from complete ruin in this year (1494) by the warnings of Savonarola, made fully four years before. In spite of what seems to have been the obvious lesson of this experience of Florence as seen by Ficino—that moral reform and purity of living might avert or put an end to calamities—Ficino curiously clung to the helpless attitude that calamities were necessary because of human weakness and could be avoided by "no virtue of ours at all," [27] since "mortals certainly are so dull that they recognize good by no other way at all except from comparison with evils." [28]

Divine justice was also held to be the explanation of the calamities by Giovanni Battista Spagnuoli (1448-1516) of Mantua in a treatise on *The Calamities of His Times and both Their Causes and Remedies* [29] printed for the first time in the same year as Ficino wrote his letter, 1494. What was frequently explained as the force of the stars, or of fortune or

24 *Ibid.*, p. 194 in a passage cited by Bandini from "*Epistolae,* Lib. II, f. 186."

25 Letter to Giovanni Cavalcanti on *Cur Providentia permittat adversa, Opera Omnia, op. cit.,* p. 961. Written "Die xii Decembris 1494," *Ibid.,* p. 963.

26 *Ibid.*, p. 961.

27 *Ibid.*, p. 963, "nulla prorsus virtute nostra."

28 *Ibid.*, p. 962, "Mortales profecto tam hebetes sunt, ut bonum non aliunde prorsus cognoscant, quam ex comparatione malorum. . ."

29 *De suorum temporum calamitatibus earumque tum causis tum remediis,* Paris, 1494, and *Opera Omnia,* 1504, ff. 119-155. Citations from latter.

fate, or of ancient deities was actually the working of divine providence. If God did not visit ruin on his peoples occasionally, their natural torpor would make them oblivious to faith and virtue.[30] Therefore, in recent times men had witnessed the moral disintegration of Italy and the consequent political disorders, devastation of cities, shipwrecks, empty churches, idle fields, famine and suffering.[31] Unlike Ficino, Battista believed that these calamities would incite men to the moral reform necessary to cure the times. The seven sins of pride, envy, anger, cupidity, voracity, lust and irritability, which prevailed and were at the roots of the calamities, could be overcome by a renewal of virtue; God's wrath could be placated, and the times improved.[32]

In 1510 the Neapolitan historian and biographer, Tristano Caracciolo (1439?-1517?) composed a treatise on *The Variety of Fortune.*[33] Although he believes with Solomon and many other writers that all things, especially sensible and tangible things, are sought in vain, these present bad times have made this belief so certain that he can not only believe it when he reads but now see, touch and know it directly. Men of the past had suffered greatly, " nevertheless, the things which we know have happened in our age disturb and upset us far more, and molest and oppress us so much the more as they convince us that even men in the age of innocence and the saints were unhappy too. . . ." Thus, while the past could be pitied, and the present suffered, to hope for the future was a mark of stupidity. Man, himself, became a part of the general vanity of things unless he raised himself to a higher, constant, stable state of joy through obeying God's commandments. The conviction that the world was a bad and miserable place could " be linked to the memory by a display of examples." Omitting to give

30 *Ibid.,* f. 119a-b.

31 *Ibid.,* ff. 119b-122a.

32 *Ibid.,* ff. 122b-155b.

33 *De Varietate Fortunae, Rerum Italicarum Scriptores,* nuova edizione, Tomo XXII, Parte I, Bologna, 1935, pp. 73-105.

examples of ancient calamities, " we shall attempt to list those
which have happened in our kingdom and age inasmuch as,
closer to us, they may be more effective in making us careful
to know our own condition." [34]

The lesson that worldly goods and the gifts of fortune were
both useless and harmful to man in those days was driven
home by a series of tragic stories beginning with the calamities
of the House of Aragon in Naples,[35] including the misfortunes
of the Sforzas in Milan through the death of Ludovico in
1508 [36] and the trials of many of the leading noble lines of
Naples,[37] ending with the recent disasters and hardships of the
Venetians.[38] " In order to deflate our arrogance and weaken
the burning thirst for possession, we have shown the unhappy
outcome of the affairs, the pitiful deaths, not only of individuals but of numerous family lines as well, the inconstancy
of things and the varieties and changes of fortune of our
time as a monument of haughty souls, who trusted in vain
and transitory things." [39]

Five years later Italian society was still suffering from the
wave of disasters initiated with the first French invasion.
Giovanni Francesco Pico della Mirandola (1476-1533), the
nephew of the better known Giovanni, felt compelled about

34 *Ibid.*, p. 73, "Tamen longe magis movent afficiuntque quae nostra aetate
contigisse cognovimus, et tanto efficacius nos vexant et premunt, quanto in-
feliciores etiam fuisse castos illos priscos et sanctos viros, praesentia haec
arguunt . . . iugi memoria per exemplorum ostensionem . . . conemur ea,
quae hoc nostro regno atque aetate gesta sint, recensere, utpote spatiis
viciniora, quae magis nos cautos ad nostram conditionem noscendam reddere
valeant."

35 *Ibid.*, pp. 73-80.

36 *Ibid.*, pp. 80-2.

37 *Ibid.*, pp. 82-100.

38 *Ibid.*, pp. 100-04.

39 *Ibid.*, p. 104, " . . . ad nostram deprimendam insolentiam, aestuantemque
habendi sitim diluendam, eventus rerum infelices, exitus miserandos, non
modo singulorum, sed etiam numerosae gentis, instabilitatem rerum,
varietatesque fortunae vices nostrae tempestatis ostenderimus ad monimentum
superbientium animorum, vanis caducisque fidentium. . ."

1515 to state *The True Causes of the Calamities of Our Times* [40] and to combat the fatalistic theories (discussed below) that were also current. Commencing with the death of his uncle in 1494, one great man of letters after another was cut down—Hermolaus Barbarus, Politian, Merula, Bossius and others. New diseases began to attack the human body; war, famine, pestilence, earthquake, siege, sedition and intrigue went on unchecked.[41] For Francesco Pico, as for Battista Spagnuoli, there was a remedy. This was for men to recognize that divine providence was punishing them for their moral delinquency and then to turn again to virtuous living.[42] The Italians should cease quarreling among themselves and acquire the ability to fight and resist invasion.[43] There was no basis for the resigned attitude of fatalism which referred the calamities to the movements of the stars or to the whim of fortune.[44] There had been many conjunctions and eclipses in the previous century without bringing calamities and wars, " for before the advent of Charles and in the previous age Italy and almost all Europe lived in the most profound peace." [45] The astrologers were faulty in blaming the planets, " both since calamities were repeatedly seen in lands without their conjunction, and since conjunctions occurred in accordance with their calculation when nevertheless no calamities happened in the lands." [46]

The humanists who were suffering in the tragic period of the subordination of Italy to the armies of foreign rulers were not always as ready to prescribe remedies for the disasters

40 *De veris calamitatum causis nostrum temporum,* ed. Ferdinandus Caesius, Modena, 1860 from an edition of 1519. It must have been written ca. 1515 since Francesco Pico begins the period of calamities in 1494 and, p. 21, speaks of, " Horum . . . unius et viginti annorum calamitates. . ."

41 *Ibid.,* pp. 13-21.   42 *Ibid.,* capita 7, 8, 9.

43 *Ibid.,* capitum 10.   44 *Ibid.,* capita 2-6.

45 *Ibid.,* p. 27, " Nam ante Caroli adventum et priori etiam seculo in altissima pace degebat Italia, et fere omnis Europa."

46 *Ibid.,* p. 30, ". . . quandoquidem et calamitates sine eorum concursu in terris saepenumero visae et concursus ut ipsi volunt ex eorum supputatione extitit, cum nullae tamen in terris calamitates extiterunt. . ."

overwhelming society. Just as at the time when the problem of individual security seemed uppermost to the humanists, there were in this period of social and political collapse and disorder writers who felt that the adverse conditions of the world had to be accepted in resignation without much hope of turning the trend of events toward a happier state of affairs. While Ficino, or Battista Spagnuoli, or Francesco Pico were willing to entreat divine providence with the expectation that a revival of morality or piety might appease the just wrath of the Ruler of the universe, other writers believed that the ultimate cause of things was beyond their control or understanding, and that a knowledge of the character of the immediate forces controlling events was alone open to man. By understanding the working of fate, either through the stars or fortune, individual adjustments could be made in time to avert being caught personally in the calamities, but the trend of events itself could not in this way be altered. Advance knowledge of events also helped to overcome at least the mental torture of suffering from the unknown and the inexplicable. In contrast to those humanists who were willing to entrust themselves and society to providence, however, this group, which was more fatalistic about the trend of events, was pessimistic because it lacked any confidence that the world, given human willingness to conform to the purposes of the Creator, could become more favorable to the life of man. The believers in providence were less pessimistic, for even considering the foolish perversity of man in resisting divine law and the temptations of the world which were so difficult for man in his weakness to resist, there still remained the possibility that man, in respecting the moral and religious imperatives, might avoid punishment at the hands of providence.

The philosopher, Agostino Nifo (1473?-1538 or 1545), lacked confidence either in this possibility of human moral regeneration or in the power of the human mind to understand the workings of divine providence with sufficient certainty to be able to guide man's conduct in accord with it. Hence, he as-

sumed an attitude of passive acceptance of the calamities,
mitigated by whatever consolation foreknowledge of the course
of events through a knowledge of astrology might afford to
man. Writing in 1504 at Sessa in Campania, where he had
witnessed the devastation resulting from the manoeuvres and
sieges of the French and Spanish forces, he was more interested
in explaining *The Causes of Our Calamities* [47] than in pre-
scribing any very effective remedies for them. If it were possible to predict the coming of disaster, however, some consolation would be afforded, for, " no one knowing the causes
of things is astonished, no one foreseeing calamities is saddened, no one knowing unfavorable events beforehand is helpless." [48] Although he had suffered in this age, he was able to
mitigate his sorrows by knowing the future course of events,
thus avoiding many of the calamities.[49]

At one time he had enjoyed tranquillity at Padua, where
he wrote commentaries on philosophy, but the calamities which
raged in Italy for the past ten years (1494-1504) had turned
him to " another kind of writing," [50] the investigation of the
causes of calamities. They came, of course, from the anger of
God, to punish men for their wickedness. But " the human
mind grows silent when it comes to speaking about God; it
can say scarcely anything about celestial bodies but much more
easily than about God." [51] He confined himself for this reason
to the celestial causes of calamities: eclipses, conjunctions etc.
There seemed to be good reason for this procedure, for there
were ten eclipses between 1493 and 1503, and the eclipse of
the sun in 1493 was directly followed by the invasion of Italy

47 *De nostrarum calamitatum causis*, Venice, 1505, f. 1a mentions how
the Spaniards seized Sessa in 1503 and he had fled to Marseolo.

48 *Ibid.*, f. 1b, " Nemo sciens rerum causas admiratur, nemo calamitates
previdens contristatur, nemo importunos prenoscans eventus languet."

49 *Idem.*

50 *Ibid.*, f. 1a, " aliud scribendi genus."

51 *Idem.*, " De deo loqui sileat mens humana; de celestibus vix pauca
loqui potest, sed multo facilius quam de deo."

by Charles VIII in 1494.[52] After pointing out the advantages
of the knowledge astrology gave one—being able to avoid
places where trouble was expected and seek favorable spots—
he turned to the main portion of the work, a treatise on
astrology, relying mainly on Ptolemy.[53]

On December 31, 1504 an earthquake struck Bologna, Fer-
rara and Venice. It recurred several times during the first half
of 1505 causing heavy damage to buildings and great suffering, especially from the plague which broke out in Bologna
as a sequel of the earthquake. The entire city joined in pro-
cessions, pilgrimages and penitence to try to appease the wrath
of God.[54]

This disaster was the occasion for Filippo Beroaldo, whose
optimistic views on human nature have already been shown,
to emphasize his despair about human life in spite of man because of the hostility of the external world. In a treatise on
Earthquake,[55] he argued that " if man does not always suffer,
he is always likely to suffer fires, shipwrecks, floods, falling
roofs, earthquakes and six hundred other dangers of that
sort." [56] Many causes have been alleged to explain the dangers
of nature to which man is subject, such as the mixing of opposite elements, the power of the stars, or the wrath of God.[57]
But the important thing to recognize is that, whatever the
cause, such a thing as an earthquake is " an atrocious, dire,
fatal and calamitous thing." [58] His experience of calamity left
him with no remedy against it. He could only conclude, as
he did in his work on *Happiness,* that although man needed

52 *Idem.*

53 *Ibid.,* f. 1b.

54 Salvatore Muzzi, *Annali della Città di Bologna dalla sua Origine al
1796,* Bologna, 1845, vol. V, pp. 464-71.

55 *Opusculum de terraemotu,* ff. 147-52, *Varia Opuscula, op. cit.*

56 *Ibid.,* f. 147a, " Qui incendia, naufragia, praecipitia, tectorum lapsus,
tremores terrae, sexcentaque alia id genus pericula et si non semper patitus
tamen pati potest. . ."

57 *Ibid.,* ff. 147a-150b.

58 *Ibid.,* f. 150b, ". . . rem esse atrocem, diram, esitialem atque funestam."

goods of the soul, of the body and of the outer world " this gift of nature, whatever is given us, is uncertain and fragile," and that " nature, indeed, grants nothing better to men than brevity of life. . . ." [59]

In Beroaldo's discussion of *Happiness,* he attributed this unhappy state of affairs to the power of fortune, which, blind to human defects and merits, arbitrarily raised men up, only to cast them down.[60] This view was even more resigned to caprice and pessimistic than Nifo's submission to the stars, which at least showed some calculable regularity in their movements. Beroaldo's city, Bologna, was one of the objects of French, Papal, and Venetian ambition, so that Beroaldo was particularly aware of the difficulties and calamities of the times and was, perhaps, compelled to assume a resigned attitude about this life in spite of his appreciation of human nature.

Pietro Alcyonio, a Venetian humanist of the early sixteenth century, spent the greater part of his career in the service of Cardinal Giulio de' Medici, later Pope Clement VII. His attitude toward the calamities of the times was reflected through the experience of his patron. He composed a dialogue between Cardinals Giulio and Giovanni de' Medici called *The Medici Legate on Exile.*[61] The conversation must have taken place early in 1512, for Giovanni was Papal Legate at that time, and he referred hopefully to the restoration of the Medici in Florence planned by the Holy League.[62] He discussed both the unhappy effects on the individual of exile, although reading of old accounts of similar misfortune afforded some consolation to the Medici for their shabby treatment by the Floren-

---

59 *De felicitate, op. cit.,* f. 122b, "incertum ac fragile est hoc munus naturae quicquid datur nobis . . . Natura vero nihil hominibus brevitate vitae praestitit melius. . ."

60 *Ibid.,* f. 121a.

61 *Medices Legatus de Exsilio,* Venice, 1522. Reprinted by J. B. Menckenius, *Analecta de Calamitate,* Leipzig, 1707. This turned the tables on Filelfo's earlier complaint about the troubles of those whom the Medici had sent into exile in his *De Exilio.*

62 *Ibid.* (Venice edition), f. A6b.

tines,[63] and the suffering of all parts of Italy as a result of the internal disorders and foreign invasions.[64] The most tragic thing to Giovanni was that the unjust suffering of the Medici and their friends " could not be relieved except by arms, than which no kind of calamity is more pernicious." [65] The alliances recently arranged assured them of victory. " But nevertheless in the practice of such affairs much can happen which might render victory less pleasant: the slaughter of legions both of our own men and of the kings of our allies, the carnage of citizens, destructions of cities, assaults upon the fortunes of private individuals, new tables of proscriptions, honoring of the vilest." [66] Worse, these things would happen again not in the northern countries where perversity of custom or religious disunity made war necessary, " but through Italy where humanity, moderation, virtue and religion began and were thought to be spread in all lands." [67] Giovanni was saddened not only by the thought of the misery about to be unleashed but also by " the memory of the recent war. . ." [68] After a detailed description of the calamities resulting from the past eighteen years of conflict,[69] the conversation turned to examples drawn from the past of calamities suffered by noble men.[70] Although no theory

63 *Ibid.,* ff. A4b-A6b, and body of treatise.

64 *Ibid.,* ff. A6b-A7b.

65 *Ibid.,* f. A6b, " non . . . levari posse nisi armis quibus nullum calamitatis genus perniciosius est."

66 *Idem.,* " Sed tamen in talium rerum administratione multa incidere possunt quae victoriam minus laetam reddent: strages legionum tum nostrarum tum Regum sociorum, caedes civium, direptiones urbium, impetus in privatorum pecunias, tabulae novae proscriptiones, turpissimorum honores." Giovanni's conscience bothered him about the violence of the recapture of Florence until his death. Alcyonio probably composed this work after the event and was aware of the future Leo's qualms.

67 *Idem.,* ". . . sed per Italiam ubi humanitas, moderatio, virtus et religio orta et in omnes terras putatur distributa." If the reference to religious disunity meant Luther, the treatise must have been composed not long before its publication in 1522.

68 *Idem.,* " Auget dolorem mecum memoria superioris belli. . ."

69 *Ibid.,* ff. A6b-A7b.   70 *Ibid.,* ff. A7b-15a.

explaining why men had to suffer calamities was given, Alcyonio's attitude may be described as resigned to these conditions. As with Poggio,[71] this was the way of the world.[72]

Resignation and acceptance of the sad state of affairs pervaded the attitude of Giovanni Piero Valeriano also. Writing on *The Unhappiness of Men of Letters* [73] a little while after the most severe of all the calamities happening in Italy, the Sack of Rome by the Spaniards and Germans in 1527, Valeriano expressed what all the humanists, who had achieved recognition for their activities only to be engulfed in the general ruin of Italy, must have felt. " All men of letters are born for calamities and unhappiness, especially at this time." [74] His passive sorrow and deep pessimism about the future must have been extremely convincing. " But, good God," he exclaimed, " when first I began to inquire after the philosophers, orators, poets and professors of Greek and Latin letters, whom I have written about, how great and how cruel a tragedy was presented to me, for I found that the men of letters, whom I had hoped to see, had been miserably destroyed in great numbers, and subjected to the most atrocious bitterness of fate, affected by the most unworthy misfortunes, some killed by pestilence, others driven into exile and oppressed with want, these butchered by the sword, those assailed by daily torments, others, and this I think is the most atrocious of all calamities, committed suicide." [75]

71 See above, pp. 125-126.

72 It is noteworthy that Alcyonio was well provided for by his patron and hence was not concerned about his personal security but about the security of the family which was supporting him.

73 *De Litteratorum Infelicitate Libri Duo,* Geneva, 1821, also printed by Menckenius, *op. cit.*

74 *Ibid.,* (Geneva edition) p. 2, " Litteratos omnes ad aerumnias et infelicitates nasci hoc praesertim tempore."

75 *Ibid.,* p. 5, " Sed, bone Deus, cum primum caepi Philosophos, Oratores, Poetas, Graecarum Latinarumque Litterarum professores, quos in commentario conscriptos habebam, perquirere, quanta, quamque crudelis tragedia mihi oblata est, qui litteratos viros, quos me visurum sperebam, tanto numero comperiebam miserabiliter ocubuisse, atrocissimaque fati acerbitate

Valeriano was not satisfied with merely expressing his feelings about his tragic times. He devoted his entire treatise to proving his argument by giving examples of the calamities that had befallen the foremost humanists of his time. Such a remedy as to return to virtue would have been of no avail, for all of these men were of outstanding and self-evident virtue in their lives and possessed of great talent. Thus he could say with justice that " through all Europe in our age good letters are so vexed by the unkindness of the fates that there is no province, no city, no town in which for the past forty years some unheard of calamity has not weighed heavily on men of this class." Worst of all, " this tempest is poured forth even upon the best. . . ." [76] Confronted as he was with the climax of ruin, it seems only natural that there was little room in Valeriano's attitude for anything but the most bleak despair. Hope that virtue might encourage providence to bring better times seemed impossible.

Half a generation later, although the Catholic reformation had begun to draw Italian men of letters into its service, the same attitude of fatalism and helplessness pervaded the work of another author of lives of Italian humanists. Paolo Giovio's (1483-1552) *Eulogy of Learned Men* [77] was in some ways an epitaph on the miserable end of humanism in Italy. The study of letters seemed to him to have passed to the northern countries, yet he still hoped that it might persist a little in Italy. " This unkind age has not been to them so generous a

sublatos, indignissimisque affectos infortuniis, alios peste interceptos, alios in exilio, et inopia oppressos, hos ferro trucidatos, illos diuturnis cruciatibus absumptos, alios, quod aerumnarum omnium atrocissimam arbitror, ultro sibi mortem conscivisse."

76 *Ibid.*, p. 6, ". . . per universam etiam Europam aetate nostra bonas litteras ita fatorum inclementia vexatas, ut nulla provincia sit, civitas nulla, nullum oppidum, in quo quadrigesimo ad hinc anno non aliqua insignis calamitas in hoc hominum genus incubuerit . . . tempestas haec in optimos quoque effusa est. . ."

77 *Elogia doctorum virorum*, translated under title *An Italian Portrait Gallery* by Florence Alden Cragg, Boston, 1935.

mother nor to us so cruel a stepmother that she has left us nothing at all of our ancient heritage." Italians should " nobly guard what is left of the great possessions of our ancestors; though this can be but empty comfort in our miseries. . ." [78] It was indeed difficult, for the only living authors he could write about were " those whom the disasters of civil and foreign wars have spared. . ." [79] His short biographies themselves give his attitude toward the times. Camillo Querno " ended his life in a public hospital, for, indignant at the cruelty of Fortune, in despair he stabbed himself in the stomach with a pair of shears." [80] The sad fate of Alberto Pio of Carpo was " evidence of Fortune's malicious and insolent mockery of human plans." [81] Suffering the double misfortune of the loss of his patrimony and of the affliction of severe gout, " it availed him nothing that he bore it bravely with Christian patience and resignation. . ." [82]

It is hard to see how sixteenth century humanists, if they were at all sensitive to the trends of their times, could be anything else but profoundly embittered about the future of Italian society. Those that looked upon the adversities as the results of fate, against which human efforts were of little avail, were in one sense corroborated by the future. Although the political instability of the Italian states was eventually resolved, and war and invasion with their mass horrors became less of a daily condition, nevertheless Italy never fully recovered its previous prosperity and its leading position culturally and economically in Europe. On the other hand, the humanists who looked to moral revival as a remedy against providential anger were also to some extent prophetic in their point of view. Certainly in the second half of the sixteenth and in the seventeenth century what little support was available for humanistic

78 *Ibid.*, p. 167.
79 *Ibid.*, p. 170.
80 *Ibid.*, p. 118.
81 *Idem.*
82 *Ibid.*, p. 119.

cultivation of *belles lettres* and the classics could be found as much in Rome among the satellites of the papal curia as anywhere in Italy. The blows of providence fell less heavily in actual fact upon those in Italy who thenceforth tried to strengthen and reinforce the influence of the Church. Yet the comparative optimism of these trusters in providence was probably less realistic than the pessimism and resignation of the fatalistic humanists. More important than the specific attitude of the humanists, providential or fatalistic, was the fact that at this time in the history of the humanists as a whole, many of them were so strongly impressed with the critical problem which the calamities of the period thrust upon them. Whether they believed that something could be done or not, they were forced to recognize that they were involved and could not escape or make exceptions for themselves. One's personal virtue might have brought consolation for one's shortcomings socially, but it could not cleanse the cities of pestilence nor clear the fields of invaders. Whether they liked it or not, the humanists were now part of society and had to rise or fall with society itself. Even in this situation they thought more of the effect upon themselves of the fate of society than of the fate of society itself.

CHAPTER VI
SOME AFTERTHOUGHTS

ONLY a very small portion of the material that has been examined applied to the fourteenth century humanists so that no very reliable conclusions can be drawn about this early period. The attitudes of Petrarch and Salutati alone of the early humanists were investigated. They were influenced by Stoicism in their points of view, and they were included among representatives of this influence in order to illustrate this tendency of humanist thought. They did show that the theories of this school of philosophy were not determinative in shaping the humanists' ideas, since they neither consistently practiced the teachings of the Stoics nor absolutely accepted them in theory. Neither Petrarch nor Salutati completely forswore positions of wealth. They were usually uncertain about the correct course to pursue and wavered from time to time. While Petrarch was especially insecure about life, Salutati more and more emphasized the Christian teaching of love in his writings, while maintaining an exterior bearing of austerity. He was closer in practice to the Stoic ideal than Petrarch, whose warm emotional reactions conformed more with Christianity. The very inconsistency of these two humanists makes it difficult to discover any clear explanation for their ideas.

Moreover the variety of attitudes of fifteenth century humanists also makes flat judgments about this later period difficult. There was a Stoic tendency that was tolerant of some human activities in the sense that it believed that a man could through reason secure repose in this life. The same writers, however, modified this view by emphasizing the difficulties and rarity of anyone achieving security in this way. In another sense they were also resigned to unhappiness because they believed that worldly activities disturbed man's composure and that the effort to overcome the desire for wealth or fame was on the other hand equally upsetting. There was another group, Christian or Neoplatonist in its theories, which was fearful of both worldliness and the victory of reason in this life. Writers of this school were sustained by the hope of a future life for the virtuous man, but they modified their otherworldly expectations by recognizing the difficulties in the way of becoming virtuous. There was finally another bloc, Aristotelian or Epicurean in doctrine, which admitted the place of both virtue and worldly success in this life and believed that the achievement of both was possible. Such writers were more consistently appreciative of human values, although they believed that happiness in this life was sometimes subordinate to hope for a future reward, and that sometimes it was difficult to be both virtuous and prosperous. It is even more difficult to find any consistency in the attitudes of fifteenth century humanists than of fourteenth century writers, though there is much more to base a conclusion on. The only thread of uniformity running through their ideas is their concern with the common problem of how individual man can make a happy adjustment to life both in this world and the next.

It is very nearly as difficult to find any uniformity if the fifteenth century is divided into smaller periods in order to trace a development or transition of opinions through successive intervals. The different tendencies are distinguishable only in their emphases; no sharp line can be drawn between the Stoic, Christian, Neoplatonist, Aristotelian and Epicurean directions which seem to run logically into each other in this order. Thus even if the tendencies were concentrated at different time-intervals, development would be scarcely discernible except in the philosophies to which lip service was given. The first half of the century seems, because of the recent influence of Petrarch and especially Salutati, to be more Stoic than the second half. Yet Platina was a Stoic in the eighties. Bruni and Valla, whose views were most opposed to Stoicism, flourished in the second quarter of the century. Platonism, on the other hand, was cultivated more vigorously in the second half of the century. Perhaps this indicates that the humanists were more readily received in wealthy circles so that the contrast between the classical scholar and the man of worldly affairs was not so sharp as it had been earlier, and both types of life were less distinguishable also in regard to virtue and happiness than Stoicism tended to make them. The actual theories of the humanists of Stoic tendency, however, blunted the sharpness of the distinction made by the original philosophy and came very close to the attitudes of the Neoplatonists. If there was any development, it was slight and almost imperceptible. There seems to be almost as much of a mixture of opinions for any part as for the century as a whole.

The period of invasions beginning in 1494 and continuing through the first third of the sixteenth century seemed to bring increasing attention to the conditions of the times on the part of the humanists. This was a shift from the earlier concern with the problems of the individual or of generic man in the abstract. It cannot be claimed with any assurance that such a shift of perspective was universal, however, since only the literature on the calamities was especially sought for this period. Those humanists who felt that the future of their times was in the hands of providence were rather more hopeful of a good end than those who accepted the disasters as the work of fate, since the former group felt that moral improvement could be an effective remedy, while the latter group saw no remedy and could only offer, in one case, whatever consolation or practical help in avoiding calamities foreknowledge through astrology might afford. The feeling of helplessness was not always overcome by the believers in providence, for Ficino, at least, saw no remedy and looked only to divine mercy to give warnings at such times. Whatever explanation was made or remedy proposed, the fear and dread of the effects of the catastrophes inflicted both by man and nature during this period were universal.

In general little uniformity can be found in the attitude of the Italian humanists toward the problems of existence. Doubt must be thrown upon efforts to find in the attitudes of the humanists any broad characteristics with which to stamp the historical period in which they were active as distinct from the Middle Ages. Apart from the generally recognized error of exaggerating the importance of the humanists in the culture or in the intellectual life of this period, it is also a mistake to think of them as being onesidedly enthusiastic about life or, on the other hand, as being generally infected with resignation for whatever reason. Their actual attitudes range from the partially pessimistic to the partially optimistic with many points of view that defy classification and with inconsistencies and variations in the attitudes of particular individuals. The more despondent tendencies have been emphasized not for the sake of claiming that they were closer to the actual position of the humanists in general, but largely because a false emphasis upon their happier and more confident moods has been common. Other historians, including Burckhardt, have recognized that there was a gloomy side to the thought of the period, but while recognizing that the humanists had their moments of doubt and uncertainty, it has been usual to depict the brighter, optimistic moods as the normal. The problem, however, is not so simple of solution, and despair about this life should not be considered quite so exceptional.

If it seems that there was no single outlook on life that characterized the humanists, or no uniform development in the history of their outlook, it does not mean that there was no homogeneity in the lives of the humanists. They responded in a series of different ways, which have been set forth, to a problem which they all seemed to face, namely, how was a writer to find some meaning in his life's work when the world in which he lived increasingly valued the material things, which came as a reward to the fortunate man of affairs, more than the permanent things of beauty or truth or goodness which seemed to come from study. Probably, and nothing but pure conjecture is possible here, a person became a humanist in the first place because he associated the study of the classics and of *belle lettres* with enduring values, considering them more important than the struggle for material reward. And perhaps the idealization of the thought and literature of the remote ancient world implied a criticism of and a pessimism about his own world. The pity of it for him was that he couldn't avoid living in his own world.

This conjecture implies that there was an element of idealism in the original motives of the humanists, but it does not mean that they had to cling to their original lofty ideals once they were launched on a career, nor that idealism and a desire for self-glorification, best achieved through accomplishments in the field of highest values, were incompatible. Quite the contrary, the conditions of the societies in which the humanists lived made the injection of sordid elements and selfish motives into their lives inevitable. Unless one came from a well-endowed family, the devotion to these putative superior values had to be interrupted or compromised by the pursuit of material support in one form or another. For the poor humanist, there was an inescapable conflict between his ideal and the practical necessities of life. The study of the humanities was pursued because it seemed uncontaminated by the harsh world of business or politics, yet studies could not be pursued without recourse either to personal participation in the sordidness of making a fortune or a position or to sycophancy and flattery of a magnate or prince who was thoroughly soiled.

Only certain solutions were possible, given this conflict. Such a humanist might have pretended that the gifts he received from a patron were really quite indifferent as far as affecting his own inner composure, which he gained from practicing virtue—humanism—while abstaining personally from the business or political worlds. He could be nicely inconsistent in his theories and his actual mode of life with this solution. Another solution might have been to the effect that humanism, although of greater value than mere worldly success, was itself but the means toward some future higher end, realizable only in the next life and that the study of secular letters had to be secondary to the study of divine matters. It was then no compromise for him to seek a patron of wealth, since there was not the same high ideal to compromise. He could also be realistic and believe that a little wealth never hurt a humanist and that it was a practical necessity for carrying on humanism. This was an honest compromise, and a solution which eliminated the possibility of theory being violated by practice, provided, of course, that the study of the humanities was not altogether abandoned for the pursuit of this world's goods. In all three solutions, a sub-problem was also taken care of. How could these men write in praise of their ideal of humanism and not offend the great men from whom they were forced to seek rewards? In the second and third solutions the worldly activities of the great were either made to seem little worse ultimately than humanism or were justified as making possible the greater activities of the humanist. In the first case, the more subtle kind of flattery and favor-seeking was practiced of making the benefactor feel that his gift was a free, unsought one to the completely pure and unseeking scholar.

The humanist of wealthy or influential background also faced the same problem in a slightly altered form. The conflict in his case was between his ideal and a background which compromised him as far as his ideal was concerned. It was not fraught with quite the immediate necessity that faced the poor writer, for the wealthier one could always support himself, but emotionally it did involve him in the question of whether he should go on enjoying the benefits of his wealth now that he was becoming a humanist or whether he should emulate St. Francis and try to practice humanism in rags. His choice could be guessed in most cases, but still he had to show that he had not compromised his ideal just as the poor humanist had to do. The three solutions of the poor scholar would work just as well for him. He had the additional advantage of not having to justify the pursuit of wealth but merely the consumption of it.

These three solutions to this problem which faced the humanists were of course the three positions that they have been shown, with minor variations, expressing; namely the

Stoic, the Christian-Neoplatonist, the Aristotelian-Epicurean. So although their ideas varied widely at all times, making it difficult to characterize them, in any single way, by their theories or attitudes, they, nevertheless, did form a unified group in terms of the problem which they faced. The lack of uniformity in their ideas may be explained by the different solutions that were possible to this problem. It is notable that the problem rather than the solution was dictated by the historical conditions facing the humanist. It made little difference whether he was rich or poor, citizen or vagabond, since the same theoretical solutions worked for both. The question of the inconsistency between the ideas and the behavior of the humanists also seems to dissolve. The inconsistency simply mirrored the problem which they faced. It was impossible to be a pure humanist and to go on living. One had to compromise. The inconsistency disappeared when the compromise was honestly and realistically recognized as in Bruni's or Valla's optimistic solutions. It was perpetuated as the fact of the compromise was glossed over, explained away or ignored in the solutions of others.

Two very large questions, however, must still remain unsolved. The first is why one originally became a humanist. It was assumed above that humanism had to be idealized if one were to become such a person, and that assumption would hold good no matter what the motives might have been for believing that humanism was in some way higher than shoemaking. The other question is why a given humanist might lean toward one rather than another particular solution of the great problem which they faced. Perhaps the answer to both questions lies in the character of the person about to become a humanist, but it would be difficult to say with any accuracy what particular traits of character would influence a particular choice. It would seem, however, that the traits that led one to become a humanist most clearly and with least contradiction of motives would predispose the person toward either of the solutions which denied value to worldly goods and activities, since the original interest in humanism was also such a denial of worldly values. These two solutions excluded certain aspects of life, and so if the motives that led men to become humanists were clear and uncontradictory, there would have been good reason for a predominance of anti-human feeling among the humanists.

Unfortunately, evidence on the characters of the humanists would be extremely hard to collect, and their motives were naturally complicated by many factors not directly concerned in their solution to the problem. The age of the humanist, for example, may have made some difference in the solution favored, since the hard, restrictive solutions would seem to rest more easily on an old man with his life behind him, with little to lose, and about to die. But on the other hand, the old man might cherish the high ideals of his youth less after a life of varied experience and so be ready for an easier acceptance of the place of material values in a humanist's career. There is some evidence on this point. Filelfo, as has been seen, considered his own old age as a factor in the more rigorous and pessimistic view he then set forth.[1] Petrarch, also, became more convinced of the inferiority and evil of worldly goods in his later years.[2] Salutati, however, relaxed the vigor of his ascetic viewpoint as he grew older.[3] Bruni grew up under Salutati's frigid eye but later in life turned away from the Stoic theories to the more broadly human Aristotelian views.[4] Valla commenced life as an optimist.[5] Poggio, apparently, remained resigned to unhappiness to the end.[6] Thus it would seem that

1 See above, p. 99.

2 See above, p. 85, and Baron, *op. cit.*, pp. 6-12.

3 See above, p. 58, and Von Martin, I, pp. 82-92.

4 He was in the fifties when he translated the *Nicomachean Ethics* and wrote his *Isagogicon*. See above, p. 113, and Baron, *Leonardo Bruni Aretinos Humanistische-Philosophische Schriften*, p. 20.

5 He was twenty-four in 1431.

6 *De nobilitate* and *De infelicitate principum* were written in 1440 at the age of sixty, *De miseria humanae conditionis* in 1455 at seventy-five. Walser, *op. cit.*, however, felt that he was consistently pessimistic throughout his life.

the factor of age might work in either direction or be quite neutral in its effect. The individual circumstances of the humanist's life would have to be studied in great detail before it could be known how far any such factor as age might influence his point of view, since it would make a great difference in an old man's feeling if he had experienced a contented middle age and a turbulent youth instead of the reverse, for example.

Another factor that may have influenced the solution favored by a humanist was the element of conventionality. Perhaps, it was the proper thing for a man of letters to discourse in large terms about human happiness and to strike a pose of world-weariness and *ennui*. His treatises would then merely consist of repeating empty formulae and going through a predetermined series of motions. It is perfectly true that there is a sameness and a lack of originality about the writing of the humanists. It has already been indicated that their ideas tended to merge and lose their distinctness.[7] Nevertheless, the three points of view that have been noticed in the humanists were different enough from each other to leave some room for the personal motives of a writer to break through the shell of conventionality. He might have repeated the same arguments that many other humanists had used on behalf of the theory and solution he had elected, but the element of election remained. Thus, it may be recalled that the three treatises on *Nobility* [8] use the same arguments and reach the same conclusion, with slightly greater originality on Poggio's part than on the others. Yet their views are definitely different from Bruni's *Isagogicon*. The works of Fazio and Manetti on *The Dignity and Excellence of Man,*[9] on the other hand, copy each other in many details, but reach different conclusions because of the emphasis and weight given particular arguments. There was certainly conventionality in the mechanics of the humanists' arguments and a large amount of repetition of examples, stories, citations.

7 See above, pp. 119-120.
8 See above, pp. 48-56.
9 See above, pp. 63-77.

Their external originality was small. They were original, however, in the sense that they chose one rather than some other
thoroughly conventional point of view in order to convey their
answers to the problem which faced them. Their literary ideals
did not value originality as highly as, say, the romanticists'
later did. In fact, the humanists' conception that enduring values
could be found in the study of letters and particularly ancient
letters indicates a veneration for authority and makes repetition and citation of the same phrases from the same writers
over and over again the proper method of writing. It is noteworthy, however, that they were not too anxious to rely on
the authority of each other, for much of their repetition of
each other went completely unacknowledged. Their discussions
of the *Supreme Good,* of *Nobility,* of the *Dignity of Man* and
other themes did tend to form genres, because they were attempts to answer a common problem which all faced. Self-
expression and an unconscious sincerity which betrays the
writer's individual motives are quite possible within a genre.
The factor of conventionality, then, would seem to have played
but a minor part and was not necessarily decisive in influencing
the views set forth by individual humanists.

In fact, it seems likely that such broad questions as why men
chose to be humanists and why humanists chose to write in a
sad or happy vein can very rarely be answered when complete
and detailed autobiographical material is lacking. What can be
said and must be emphasized is that the Italian humanists had
several different points of view on their own best relationship
to life and that pessimistic points of view played a relatively
large part, large enough to make the humanists seem very
similar in outlook to some of their medieval predecessors even
though the problem the humanists faced tended to be individual
while the medieval writer faced a corporate problem. It is true
enough that many of the humanists were confronted with a
different situation than many medieval writers, but it is also
true that the same theories served to interpret both situations.

BIBLIOGRAPHY

WORKS CITED

I. MODERN WRITERS

Hans Baron, "Franciscan Poverty and Civic Wealth as Factors in the Rise of Humanistic Thought," *Speculum*, XIII, 1, January, 1938, pp. 1 ff.

——, *Leonardo Bruni Aretinos Humanistische-Philosophische Schriften,* Leipzig, 1928.

Edwyn Bevan, *Stoics and Sceptics,* Oxford, 1913.

John Elof Boodin, *Three Interpretations of the Universe,* vol. I of *God and Creation,* New York, 1934.

Walter L. Bullock, Review of Hans Baron, *Leonardo Bruni Aretino . . .,* *Speculum*, IV (1929), pp. 476-83.

Jacob Burckhardt, *Die Cultur der Renaissance in Italien,* Leipzig, 1860. Zweite durchgesehene auflage, Leipzig, 1869 used. References to English translation are to S. G. C. Middlemore's translation, fourth edition, London, 1898.

Edwin Arthur Burtt, *The Metaphysical Foundations of Modern Physical Science,* New York, 1925.

Ernst Cassirer, *Individuum und Kosmos in der Philosophie der Renaissance. Studien der Bibliothek Warburg,* X, Leipzig and Berlin, 1927.

Alfred Doren, "Fortuna im Mittelalter und in der Renaissance", pp. 71-144, *Vorträge der Bibliothek Warburg,* Teil I, Hamburg, 1922-23.

Carlo Errera, "Le 'Commentationes Florentinae de Exilio' di Francesco Filelfo," *Archivio Storico Italiana,* Series 5, Tomo 5 (1890), pp. 193-227.

Adolf Harnack, *Lehrbuch der Dogmengeschichte,* Freiburg i.B., 1890.

Kenneth Escott Kirk, *The Vision of God, the Christian Doctrine of the Summum Bonum,* Bampton Lectures for 1928, London, 1931.

Paulus Oscarius Kristeller, *Supplementum Ficinianum,* Florence, 1937.

Friederich Loofs, *Leitfaden zum Studien der Dogmengeschichte,* fourth edition, Halle, 1906.

Arthur O. Lovejoy, *The Great Chain of Being, A Study of the History of an Idea,* Cambridge, Mass., 1936.

Maurice Magendie, *La politesse mondaine et les théories de l'honnêteté en France au XVIIᵉ siècle, de 1600-1660,* Paris, 1925.

Girolamo Mancini, "Alcune Lettere di Lorenzo Valla," *Giornale Storico della letteratura italiana,* XXI (1893), pp. 1-48.

——, *Vita di Lorenzo Valla,* Florence, 1891.

Alfred von Martin, *Mittelalterliche Welt-und-Lebensanschauung in Spiegel der Schriften Coluccio Salutatis,* Munich and Berlin, 1913.

——, *Coluccio Salutati und das Humanistische Lebensideal, Beitrage zur Kulturgeschichte des Mittelalters und der Renaissance,* vol. 23, Leipzig and Berlin, 1916.

Salvatore Muzzi, *Annali della Città di Bologna dalla sua Origine al 1796,* Bologna, 1845.

Howard Rollin Patch, "The Tradition of the Goddess Fortuna in Medieval Philosophy and Literature", pp. 179-234, *Smith College Studies in Modern Languages*, vol. III, Northampton, 1922.

Edward Motley Pickman, *The Mind of Latin Christendom*, vol. I, New York, 1937.

Vittorio Rossi, *Il Quattrocento*, Milan, 1897-8.

Edward William Strong, *Procedures and Metaphysics*, Berkeley, 1936.

John Addington Symonds, *The Revival of Learning*, vol. II of *The Renaissance in Italy*, revised edition, London, 1898.

Heinrich Thode, *Franz von Assisi und die Anfänge der Kunst der Renaissance in Italien*, second edition, Berlin, 1904.

Lynn Thorndike, *Science and Thought in the Fifteenth Century*, New York, 1929.

Girolamo Tiraboschi, *Storia della letteratura italiana*, Rome, 1782-5.

Ernst Troeltsch, "Renaissance und Reformation," *Gesammelte Schriften*, Tübingen, 1923, vol. IV, pp. 270 ff.

——, *Die Soziallehren der christlichen Kirchen und Gruppen, Gesammelte Schriften*, third edition, Tübingen, 1923, vol. I.

Karl Vossler, *Die Philosophischen Grundlagen zum "süssen neuen stil,"* Heidelberg, 1904.

Ernst Walser, *Poggius Florentinus Leben und Werke, Beiträge zur Kulturgeschichte des Mittelalters und der Renaissance*, vol. 14, Leipzig and Berlin, 1914.

Max von Wolff, *Lorenzo Valla Sein Leben und Seine Werke*, Leipzig, 1893.

Gasparo Zonta, *Francesco Zabarella, 1360-1417*, Padua, 1915.

II. MEDIEVAL AND HUMANIST WRITERS AND WORKS

Pietro Alcyonio, *Medices Legatus, sive de Exsilio Libri Duo*, Venice, 1522, and in Johannes Burchardus Menckenius, *Analecta de Calamitate*, Leipzig, 1707.

Thomas Aquinas, *The Summa Contra Gentiles of St. Thomas Aquinas*, English translation by the English Dominican Fathers, vol. III, London, 1928.

Augustinus Aurelius, *De Civitate Dei Libri XXII*, English translation by Marcus Dods in Philip Schaff, editor, *A Select Library of the Nicene and Post-Nicene Fathers of the Christian Church*, Buffalo, 1887, vol. II.

Filippo Beroaldo, *De Felicitate Opusculum*, Bologna, 1495 and *Oratio de Foelicitate* in *Opuscula Varia Philippi Beroaldi*, Basel, 1513, f. cxii-cxxii.

——, *Opusculum de Terraemotu* in *Opuscula Varia, op. cit.*, f. cxlvii-clii.

Matteo Bosso, *De Tolerandis Adversis Dialogus* in *Recuperationes Fesulanae*, Florence, 1492?.

Leonardo Bruni, *Isagogicon Moralis Disciplinae* in Baron, *Leonardo Bruni Aretinos Humanistische-Philosophische Schriften, op. cit.*, pp. 20-41.

——, *De Nobilitate*, s.l.a. False attribution, see Buonaccorso da Montemagno, Jr., *Ibid.*

Tristano Caracciolo, *De Varietate Fortunae, Rerum Italicarum Scriptores,* nuova edizione, Tomo XXII, Parte I, Bologna, 1935, pp. 73-105.

Lapo da Castiglionchio, Jr., *De Curiae Romanae Commodis,* edited by R. Scholz, *Quellen und Forschungen aus Italienischen Archiven,* XVI, Rome, 1913-14.

Pandolfo Collenuccio, *Misopenes, Opere,* Bari, 1929, vol. II.

Lothario Conti (Innocent III), *De Contemptu Mundi seu de Miseria Humanae Conditionis Libri Tres* in J. P. Migne, *Patrologiae Cursus Completus. Series Latina,* vol. 217, Paris, 1855, cols. 701-746.

Giovanni Conversino, *De Miseria Humanae Conditionis,* Codex IX, 11, ff. 55v-57v of the Querini-Stampaglia library, Venice, as cited by Baron, *Speculum,* XIII, p. 12.

Giovanni Corsi, *Vita Ficini,* edited by M. A. Bandini in Galetti, *Philippi Villani Liber de Civitatis Florentiae Famosis Civibus... et de Florentinorum Litteratura Principes fere Synchroni Scriptores,* Florence, 1847.

Gregorius Crispus, *De Cultu Humanitatis et Honestatis Libellus,* Cod. Laur. Plut. 77, 17 as cited by Thorndike, *op. cit.,* pp. 181-85.

Bartolommeo Fazio, *De Excellentia et Praestantia Hominis,* in Felino Sandeo, *De Regibus Siciliae et Apuliae Epitome,* Hanover, 1611, pp. 149-68.

——, *De Viri Felicitate, seu Summi Boni Fruitione,* Leyden, 1628 and *De Vitae Felicitate* in *Dialogi Decem Variorum Auctorum,* s.l. 1473.

Marsilio Ficino, *Argumentum de Summo Bono,* in P. O. Kristeller, *Suplementum Ficinianum, op. cit.,* vol. II, pp. 96-7.

——, *Epistolae:*

"Cur Providentia Permittat Adversa," *Opera Omnia,* second edition of Henricpetri, Basel, 1576, p. 961 ff.

"Quid est felicitas, quod habet gradus, quod est aeterna," *Ibid.,* pp. 662-65.

Passage from letter cited by Bandini, editor of Corsi, *Vita Ficini,* in Galetti, *op. cit.,* p. 194, note 1 from *Epistolae Ficini,* Lib. II, f. 186.

——, *Sermoni morali della stultitia et miseria degli uomini,* Codex Riccardianus 2684, membr., s. xv and Codex Magliabecchianus, VI, 238, cart., misc. s. xv, ff. 215-227v according to Kristeller, *op. cit.,* vol. I, p. xx. These sermons are Italian translations from Latin letters cited from *Opera Omnia, op. cit.* by Kristeller and in text p. 103, note 83.

——, *De Voluptate, Opera Omnia, op. cit.,* vol. I, pp. 986-1012.

Francesco Filelfo, *Commentationes Florentinae de Exilio Libri Tres,* Cod. Magliab. VI, 209 (II, 70), autograph. Cited Errera, *op. cit.*

——, *De Morali Disciplina Libri Quinque,* Venice, 1552.

Paolo Giovio, *Elogia Doctorum Virorum,* Basel, 1577. English translation by Florence Alden Cragg as *An Italian Portrait Gallery,* Boston, 1935.

Index of Council of Trent, *Index Librorum Prohibitorum cum Regulis Confectis per Patres a Tridentino Synodo delectos Auctoritate Pii IIII Primum editus,* Rome, 1596.

Cristoforo Landino, *Disputationum Camaldulensium Libri Quattuor,* Venice, 1500.

Gianozzo Manetti, *De Dignitate et Excellentia Hominis Libri Quatuor*, Basel, 1532.

Lorenzo de' Medici, *Lauda I*, " O Dio, o sommo bene, or come fai? ", *Opere*, Florence, 1825, vol. III, pp. 79-82.

Buonaccorso da Montemagno, Jr., *Leonardo Aretini Opusculum . . . de Nobilitate*, s.l.a.   Attributed to Buonaccorso in other editions and rightly according to Baron, *Leonardo Bruni* etc., *op. cit.*, pp. 180 ff.

Giovanni Nesi, *De Moribus*, Cod. Laur. Plut. 77, 24 as cited by Baron, *Speculum*, XIII, p. 25 and Thorndike, *op. cit.*, pp. 187-91.

Agostino Nifo, *De Nostrarum Calamitatum Causis*, Venice, 1505.

Matteo Palmieri, *Della Vita Civile*, edited Milan, 1830.

Francesco Petrarca, *Secretum de Contemptu Mundi*, Strassburg, 1473, English translation by W. H. Draper as *Petrarch's Secret or the Soul's Conflict with Passion*, London, 1911.

——, *De Vita Solitaria*, English translation by Jacob Zeitlin as *The Life of Solitude*, Urbana, 1924.

Giovanni Pico della Mirandola, *De Hominis Dignitate, Opera Omnia*, Basel, 1572, vol. I, pp. 313-31.

Giovanni Francesco Pico della Mirandola, *De Veris Calamitatum Causis Nostrarum Temporum*, edited by Ferdinandus Caesius, Modena, 1860 from an edition of 1519.

Platina (Bartolommeo de Sacchi), *De Falso et Vero Bono Dialogi Tres* in *De Vitis ac Gestis Summorum Pontificum . . . Eiusdem item Platinae . . .*, Cologne, 1551.

——, *De Vera Nobilitate*, in *De Vitis ac Gestis . . . op. cit.*

Giovanni Poggio Bracciolini *De Infelicitate Principum, Opera Omnia*, Basel, 1538, pp. 390-419.

——, *De Miseria Humanae Conditionis Libri Duo, Opera Omnia, op. cit.*, pp. 88-131.

——, *De Nobilitate, Opera Omnia, op. cit.*, pp. 64-83.

Coluccio Salutati, *De Saeculo et Religione*, Codex Laur. Plut. 53, 4, f. 260 ff. as cited by von Martin, *Mittelalterliche* etc., *op. cit.* and Baron, *Speculum*, XIII, p. 16; edited by T. F. Rich and B. L. Ullmann, *Bibliotheca Scriptorum Medii Recentisque Aevorum*, Leipzig, 1934.

——, *Epistolario di Coluccio Salutati*, edited by F. Novati in *Archivio della Societa Romana di storia patria*, vols. XV-XVII, Rome, 1891-6.

Oliver of Siena, *De Deo et Rerum Naturalium Principiis et Summa Beatitudine*, Cod. Laur. Plut. 82, 21 as cited by Thorndike, *op. cit.*, pp. 191-3.

Giovanni Battista Spagnuoli, *De Suorum Temporum Calamitatibus Earumque tum Causis tum Remediis*, Paris, 1494 and *Opera Omnia*, 1504, ff. 119-55.

Giovanni Piero Valeriano, *De Litteratorum Infelicitate Libri Duo*, Geneva, 1821 and in J. B. Menckenius, *Analecta de Calamitate, op. cit.*

Lorenzo Valla, *De Voluptate ac Vero Bono Libri Tres*, Basel, 1519 and in *Opera Omnia*, Basel, 1540.

Mafeo Vegio, *De Felicitate et Miseria Dialogus,* in *Dialogi Decem Variorum Auctorum,* s.l., 1473.

Vespasiano da Bisticci, *Vite di uomini illustri del secolo XV,* English translation by William George & Emily Waters as *The Vespasiano Memoirs,* London, 1926.

Francesco Zabarella, *De Felicitate Libri Tres,* Padua, 1655.

INDEX

Adjustment to life, aided by idea of ethical nobility, 49-50

Age, influence on attitude of humanists difficult to show, 148-149

Agriculture, healthy but consumes energy, 54

Albertus Magnus, as neo-semi-Pelagian, 20n

"Alcune Lettere di Lorenzo Valla", (v. Mancini)

Alcyonio, Pietro, *Medices Legatus de Exsilio*, 46 & n, 135-137; reflects fate of patrons in attitude on calamities, 135

Alexander of Hales, as neo-semi-Pelagian, 20n

Alfonso of Naples, 77n

Alliance of Florence, Milan, Naples, 126

Aloofness, and introversion required by Filelfo, 99-100; of humanists and spiritualism of ideas, 83

Altruism, a modern attitude, 17; as means to enjoyment, 114-115

Ambition, perils of and weakness of man should lead to suppression of desire, 85-86

Ambrose, Manetti proposes to refute, 73

Analecta de Calamitate (v. Menckenius)

Ancient deities, not true cause of calamities, 129

Ancient writers, selected for otherworldly ethics, 57-58

Annali della Città di Bologna (v. Muzzi)

Anxieties of men, will disappear in next life, 76

Apathy, of Stoics and humility of Christians, 58

Aquinas, compared with humanists, 37-38; contrasted with Augustine, 36-38; happiness achieved socially, 35; happiness in contemplation of truth, 34; happiness not in bodily goods, 33; happiness not in goods of chance, 32-33; happiness not in pleasures of body, 32; happiness not in will or feeling, 32; happiness of beatific vision, 35-36; happiness of intelligent substance in knowing God, 31; no happiness through senses, 33; no happiness

through virtues, 33; on importance of all human activity, 36-37; privileged status of theologian, 36; represents one phase of medieval thought, 31; *Summa Contra Gentiles*, 31-36; theories of happiness compared to Ficino's, 102-103; views happiness metaphysically, 31

Aragon, Neapolitan house of, calamities of, 130

Argumentum de Summo Bono (v. Ficino)

Aristocratic aloofness, of educated man, 60

Aristocratic attitude, consolation for insecurity, 62-63

Aristocratic character, of humanists' ideal of nobility, 57

Aristocratic intellectualism, in Aquinas, 34

Aristotle, 103; cited on human mind, 74; followed by Bruni, 111-112; Manetti proposes to refute, 73; *Nichomachean Ethics*, 109; on need of wealth for virtue, 51; refuted on definition of nobility, 55

Aristotelian influence on 15c humanism, 142

Aristotelianism, Bruni, 109; reason as moderator of soul, 81-82

Aristotelians, 21, 23; criticized by Augustine, 25; view of creation rejected, 65

Arno valley, flood of, 126

Artisan, not noble, 53

Astrologers, errors in explaining calamities, 131

Astrology, as aid to withstanding calamities, 133

Augustine, 96; admiration of beauties and blessings of nature, 29; admiration of human body, 29, human mind, 28; admired by Petrarch, 84; and otherworldliness of humanists, 92-93; as spokesman of Petrarch's conscience, 85-86; attitude related to works on *Dignity of Man*, 64; contrasted with Aquinas, 36-38; critique of Aristotelians and Platonists, 25; critique of Stoics, 24; *De Civitate Dei*, 22-29; describes calamities of this world, 27; describes human errors, 26; describes miseries of life, 24; dis-

variety of brings calamities, 129-130; (v. also Doren, Patch)
Francesco Zabarella, 1360-1417 (v. Zonta)
"Franciscan Poverty and Civic Wealth" (v. Baron)
Franciscans, follow Augustine not Aquinas, 37; influence on humanism, seen as introverting egoism, 13-14, through doctrine of poverty, 16-17
Franz von Assisi (v. Thode)
Freedom of man, in Pico, 66-67
Free will, does not bring supreme good, 50; not obstacle to suffering, 106-107
French invasion of 1494, follows break up of alliance, 126
Friendship, as love of neighbor, 60; brings praise and fame, 60; of humanists, a bond against vulgar, 60, not personal, 60-61
Fruits of men, utility of, 75
Fusion of trends among 15c. humanism, 142

Galetti, ed. *Philippi Villani Liber de Civitatis Florentinae Famosis Civibus...*, 127n
Geneva, fire of, 126
Genres, formed by humanists' treatises, 149-150
Gerbert, 10n
Giovio, Paolo, *Elogia Doctorum Virorum*, 138-139; mourns suffering of humanists and fears eclipse of humanism in Italy in calamities, 138-139
Glories of heaven, described by Manetti, 76
Gnosticism, 20
Gonzaga, Alexander, his piety, 106
Goodness of this world as means to divine end, 19
Goods of Chance, bring no happiness for Aquinas, 32-33
Great Chain of Being, The (v. Lovejoy)
Greek City-state, decline influences humanists, 40
Guiccardini, Jacopo di, 104

Happiness, Aquinas sees in beatific vision, 35-36; Aquinas sees in contemplation of truth, 34; Aquinas views as socially achieved, 35; Beroaldo's view, 117-118; Bruni's view, 109-112; Church's view, 19-20; confined to an elite by monastic and Stoic humanist theory,

93; defined as *Nobility*, 50; exceptional achievement, 89; excluded from crowd alone, 88; from otherworldliness in Pico, G., 100; gained in next life after suffering now, 106-107; human nature regarded unfavorable for, 108-109; in bodily and mental well-being, 94; in contemplation of God in next life, 102; in honesty and intelligence, 99; in moderation possible in pleasure and virtue to Valla, 116-117; in pleasure in this life, 107; in practice of virtue for Peripatetics, 110; in speculative virtues, 102; in virtues, 101; lacking to all, 88; medieval Christian view, chap. II; modern belief lies in egoism, 9; not gained through senses, 33; not gained through virtues, 33; not in bodily good, 101; not in bodily goods for Aquinas, 33; not in goods of chance for Aquinas, 32-33; not in goods of fortune, 101; not in moral virtues, 101; not in pleasures, 101; not in pleasures for Aquinas, 32; not in powers of mind, 101; not in this world, 24; not in will or feeling for Aquinas, 32; of humanists, Burckhardt's view, 9-10; of individual the concern of humanists, 5; Platina admits is in repression and contemplation, 91; possible for no one, 118; relation to *Nobility* in Platina, 50; requires bodily good and wealth, 110; requires favorable circumstances as well as virtue, 110; the supreme good, 5; Theories of Man's Fitness for, Chap. IV; through amicable social relations, theory lacking in humanists, 83; through achievement and hard work, theory lacking in humanists, 85; through contemplation, 97; through ending conflict of reason and emotion in repression or otherworldliness, 108-109; through goods of soul, body and fortune, 117; through repression of feeling in Salutati, 87; through submission to rule of virtue in Petrarch, 86; seen by Aquinas as knowledge of God, 31; seen in this life by Augustine through hope of future, 26; seen neither in virtue nor prosperity, 92; Varro's digest of pagan views, 22-23; viewed metaphysically by

Manicheanism, 20
Manuscripts cited:
Florence,
Cod. Laur. Plut. 53, 4—43n, 83n
Cod. Laur. Plut. 77, 17—49n
Cod. Laur. Plut. 77, 24—45n
Cod. Laur. Plut. 82, 21—45n
Cod. Magliab. VI, 209—45n
Cod. Magliab. VI, 238—103n
Cod. Ric. 2684—103n
Venice,
Querini-Stampaglia L i b r a r y,
Cod. IX, 11—43n
Marana, flood at, 126
Martin, Alfred von, 93, 148n; *Coluc-cio Salutati* ..., 15n, 57-63; *Mit-telalterliche Welt-und-Lebensan-schauung*, 43n, 87n; on humanism and asceticism, 14-15
Material comforts, Petrarch's atti-tudes toward, 85
Materialism, indirect argument for by Bosso, 107-108; lack of com-mon to humanists, 83
Material prosperity, difficulties of, 94; difficulties of, yet an incentive to study, 98; influence on Manetti's optimism, 77n; necessary for hap-piness, 91; Platina complains of lack of, 91
Material rewards, desired by Salu-tati, 61-62
Medices Legatus, sive de Exsilio (v. Alcyonio)
Medici, exile of, 135-137; effect on humanists, 127; restoration of, 135
Medici, Cardinal Giovanni de', 135-137
Medici, Cardinal Giulio de', 135
Medici, Cosimo de', 88n
Medici, Lorenzo de', 101, 104; Hymns of, 16; "O Dio, o summo bene ...," 44 & n
Medici, Lorenzo de', brother of Cosimo, in Poggio's dialogue *De Nobilitate*, 53-56
Medieval Catholicism, estimate of happiness, 19
Medieval Christian thought, 5, Chap-ter II
Medieval Christian ideal, retained by Salutati, 57
Medieval society, greater integration reflected in Aquinas, 37
Medieval thought, one phase repre-sented by Thomism, 31
Medieval writers, security of posi-tion, 39; similar in attitude to hu-

manists, 150; social perspective on life, 39-40
Menckenius, J. B., *Analecta de Cala-mitate*, 46n, 137n
Mental pleasures, 73
Mental powers, 96; bring no happi-ness, 101; should be employed in contemplation of divinity, 96
Merula, 131
Metaphysical Foundations of . . . Science (v. Burtt)
Middle Ages, attitudes of, difficult to distinguish humanism from, 144
Middlemore, S. G. C., trans., Burck-hardt, *The Civilisation of the Renaissance in Italy*, 9n
Migne, J. P., ed., *Patrologiae Cursus Completus*, 20n
Military life, not noble, 54
Mind, composed of fifth element, 74
Mind of man, divine origins, 74; un-able to understand Providence, 132
Misery, accompanying pursuit of worldly goods due to uncertainity of fortune, 117-118; described by Augustine, 24; limited to crowd, 88; necessity of if happiness is to be gained in next life, 106-107; of all men shown by present cala-mities, 129; of the virtuous, 105; of those who seek wealth, 92; rarely overcome, 89; universal, 88
Misery of Human Condition, not opposite theme to *Dignity of Man*, 73; refuted by Manetti, 72-76
Misopenes (v. Collenucio)
Mittelalterliche Welt-und-Lebensan-schauung ... (v. Martin)
Moderation of passion, by reason de-sirable, 111
Modesty, egoistic origins of, 115
Monastic ideal, analogous to human-ist, 14-15
Monastic state, idealized by Salutati, 58
Monasticism, conceals impotence, 115
Montemagno, Buonaccorso da, Jr., 123; *De Nobilitate*, 48-50; similar-ity to Platina, *De Vera Nobilitate*, 50; men of low birth noble, 49; nobility and virtue from own labor, 49; nobility of poor men, 49; nobil-ity of scholar, 49; noble qualities inherited, 48; wealth confers nobil-ity, 48-49
Moral philosophy, superior to science, 109
Moral purpose, conceals desire for sensual gratification, 114